# THE WINGED WHEEL PATCH

# THE WINGED WHEEL PATCH

A History Of The Canadian Military Motorcycle And Rider

•

Max Burns and Ken Messenger

**Vanwell Publishing Limited**
St. Catharines, Ontario

Canadian Cataloguing in Publication Data

Messenger, Kenneth, 1940-
The winged wheel patch
1st Canadian ed.
Includes bibliographical references and index

ISBN 0-920277-85-3

1. Motorcycles, Military - Canada. I. Burns,
Max, 1948- . II. Title.

UG620.C3M48 1993 388.3'475'0971 C-93-093451-2



Design Susan Nicholson

Vanwell Publishing Limited
1 Northrup Crescent, Box 2131
St. Catharines, Ontario L2M 6P5

Printed in Canada

Cover artwork by Sue Davies
Back Cover: Anderson, National Museums of Canada

# CONTENTS

# PREFACE

Not long into the 1900s, the motorcycle and its rider became an integral part of Canada's military establishment. This fact has largely been overlooked by both motorcycle buffs and historians. Dedicated bike enthusiasts tend to focus solely on the machine, forgetting that the motorcycle more than any other vehicle is inseparable from its operator. In motion, the two are interdependent, like Siamese twins.

Historians tend to treat both rider and machine as quaint sideshows, like the clown at a rodeo or the cartoon before the feature. Yet, as readers can judge for themselves, in the theatre of conventional warfare the motorcycle and rider formed as much a part of the feature as the tanks and infantry, the bombs and bullets, and the dead and survivors.

This book is not a review of Canada's military role in the twentieth century. Instead, it is an attempt to fill in some of the motorcycle and rider "missing links" apparent in the documentation of that history. Military motorcyclists were not usually part of prominent combat units. They were often attached to non-divisional troops such as the signals and service units, which in turn were assigned to larger formations as needed. While a regiment's history can be traced with relative ease, Despatch Riders (DRs) and other military motorcyclists became lost in the paperwork they delivered with such dedication.

In 1985, spurred into action out of our mutual interest in vintage motorcycling, we began collecting snippets of information scattered throughout countless books, dusty war diaries and memories of military riders. Originally we hoped to gather enough data to put together a cursory look at the Canadian military bike. But during the six years we ended up investing into the work, it developed into much more. We observed an overwhelming feeling among the veterans who answered our pleas for information that their contribution to their nation had been for the most part ignored. We could not help but agree.

It is not our intention to glorify these soldiers or the wars they participated in. The futility of humanity's conflicts is readily apparent. What is perhaps not so obvious is that when the veterans in this book went to war, they did so firmly believing that what they were doing was right, that the sacrifices they made were for the benefit of future generations, generations to which we and our children belong. The close comradeship that evolves from facing death with a friend, the strength of a nation united in cause, the sheer "right" of it all may never be duplicated in a nuclear age. Those who survived the wars brought back memories framed in time and injuries to a world that would not, and could not, understand.

So this has become a book with two goals: to document the history of the Canadian military motorcycle and rider in a manner we believe to be more accurate and detailed than any effort to cover the subject to date, regardless of the nation addressed, and to say thanks. No glory, just thanks.

**A few notes:**

Not all military motorcyclists were Despatch Riders (DRs). Technically speaking, Canadian DRs were riders attached to the Royal Canadian Corps of Signals (RCCS), yet the term has been universally and mistakenly applied to all military riders, even by the military itself. Therefore, we too have taken the liberty of using *DR* in the broader sense. May riders with the RCCS forgive us this one trespass.

Except where noted otherwise, all quotations are from the files of the National Archives of Canada or from the riders themselves.

# THE EARLY YEARS

The turn of the century carried the beginnings of an age of machinery into the 1900s. The fever of mechanization attacked anything that moved. Great mechanical wonders sprang forth, captivating the senses of the world. Machines of all sizes wheezed and whirred and popped and polluted. Faster trains, huge steam shovels, aeroplanes, motorcars, trucks, buses, conveyor belts, industrial tools capable of last year's impossible—the marvels were endless. In this climate of invention, it seemed only natural that someone should fit a motor to a bicycle.

Motor-cycle. Primitive technology, uncertain reliability, but what grand times were had behind the handlebars. The speed, freedom and mobility endeared these often maligned machines to the users from inception to the present.

The climate of invention that captured the citizens of this new era also found a welcome home in war. Slowly, the military powers turned to this new technology in hopes of finding that elusive advantage in battle. Significantly, the spark that ignited the world into its first global conflict was the assassination of Archduke Franz Ferdinand while he was riding in an automobile. Rapid-fire machine guns, high-explosive ammunition, aircraft bombers, fighter planes and tanks were all employed in combat for the first time. Beyond the glory-dust of gunpowder, and sometimes through its midst, passed the new cars, trucks and motorcycles.

The precedent for the motorcycle's employment in a military capacity was set by its pedal-powered ancestor. In 1875 at Somma, bicycles were put into regular service for the first time by the Italian army, delivering messages between battalions and the quartermaster-general (QM). Ten years later, England followed suit with a bicycle battalion operating in South Africa during the First Boer War. According to the British War Office, cyclists were "soldiers mounted on cycles for the purposes of locomotion and mobility," and in addition to the normal skills required by an infantryman, had to be proficient in repairs, map-reading, reconnaissance, scouting and despatch riding. Standards established later for motorcycle riders would differ little from these basics.

During the Second Boer War, some British cyclists used MMC tricycles powered by DeDion engines, while the army tested a machine-gun-equipped, motorized quadricycle known as the Simms War Machine.

Prior to the Second World War, Canada's armed forces were merely an extension of the British military. The use of motorcycles in the Canadian military was therefore officially sanctioned in 1912 when authorization for motorcycle despatch riders was granted to the Royal Engineer Signal Territorial Force in England.

Canada's pre-war commitment to military technology involved little more than observing what other countries were doing, particularly in mother Britain. Canada had neither the finances nor public support to maintain a modern army, let alone develop its own military equipment. But amid the growing talk of war during 1913, about sixty thousand Canadians volunteered for militia training, often having only the equipment they brought with them for use in the exercises. Equipment shortages were so severe that taxi cabs were occasionally employed to move troops on exercise.

It was during such training that the first use of a motorcycle in the service of the Canadian military was recorded. On 21 June 1913 the General Officer Commanding for the 2nd Division wrote to the Secretary, Militia Council, (on Military Form B.239, and no doubt in triplicate) that Pte T. Dawley, 44th Regiment (Lincoln and Welland), had been selected to serve as an orderly at the Niagara-on-the-Lake Camp HQ

> for the reason that he brought to camp with him his motor cycle. He rendered very efficient service, and did work which would have taken two mounted (cavalry) orderlies to perform.
>
> I therefore recommend that authority be granted for him to be paid the sum of $1.25 per diem (which is the rate of horse allowance) to recompense him for the use of his motor cycle in the public service.
>
> Repairs to the amount of $4.50 for piston and compensating rings, stand and frame stud, and time fitting, were necessary. I recommend that this sum also be allowed.

The request was granted and Pte T. Dawley received a grand total of $17.00. Such unquestioning generosity was to be shortlived.

From the beginning, only subalterns or NCOs were permitted to carry out their day-to-day duties on a motorcycle, a practice that has its roots in prior centuries. Traditionally, British messengers were chosen from the lower ranks because usually they were unable to read the message. Even now, a Canadian DR cannot rise above the rank of a senior NCO without giving up his mount.

Canada's unseparated close ties to its mother country also meant that when England went to war 4 August 1914, so too did Canada.

# THE FIRST WORLD WAR

The first contingent of the Canadian Expeditionary Force (CEF) disembarked in England 3 October 1914 accompanied by 9 cars, 275 bicycles and 9 motorcycles. The motorcycle that went to war in 1914 was not far removed from its bicycle heritage. The small twin coils supporting a hard leather saddle acted as the rear suspension, while front suspension, if the motorcycle had any at all, usually consisted of a crude system of pivoting rods referred to as fore-and-aft "clash" forks. Neither was overly effective, nor were the brakes, but with only 2-8 hp output from a typical one- or two-cylinder air-cooled engine, demands upon brakes were modest.

It was not unusual for early motorcycles to have bicycle-style pedals. Although handy when the engine failed to work, the pedals' primary function was to start the motor. The rider would place the motorcycle on its stand, lift the compression lever, pedal furiously, then release the compression lever. If the engine started, the bike was bounced off its stand and, if it didn't stall, the machine and rider would accelerate away. A drivebelt, one of the more reliable features of early bikes, delivered the power to the rear wheel. There was no clutch.

Multi-speed gearboxes soon became a standard feature, with the British Sturmey-Archer two- and three-speed units initially housed in the rear wheel hub (a system still used on many bicycles today). Countershaft gearboxes first appeared on American makes like the Hendee Indian, and by 1915 were nearly universal among the better-known brands.

Modifications by DRs were common. The throttle control (usually a handlebar-mounted lever that proved difficult to use over rough terrain) was often relocated, either to the handlebar end to facilitate the installation of a twist grip (as on the Indian), or to the bottom frame rails so the speed of the engine could be controlled by foot. And sometimes the gear-shift lever was moved from the side of the gas tank to the bottom of the frame, again to be operated by foot. Riders found the relocated controls much easier and quicker to operate, an important consideration when under fire. A near universal modification, usually implemented as soon as a DR took delivery of his new mount, was the removal of the muffler. This bit of motorcycle surgery made the bike sound faster to the young soldier, if not perform better.

**A Canadian DR on a Douglas Model V, Val Cartier, Quebec 1917.**

Messages were frequently delivered under cover of darkness. The bikes came equipped with acetylene lamps, which the riders used on return trips from the front, although the practice was against regulations. When a guard or officer stopped them and demanded they snuff out the light, a button operated igniter, another popular DR-installed illegal option, would shoot a spark across the lamp's burner, instantly relighting the lamp once past the guard post.

Lamps were never used when riding toward the front as the bright glare was an easy target for the enemy. For health reasons, many DRs took up smoking. The troops along the road could hear the bikes coming, but it was often too dark for either party to see. So the troops would watch for the approaching glow of a cigarette, then scurry out of the way. DRs learned to watch for three glows advancing towards them, which meant a gun carriage or an ammunition wagon with its three teams of horses was coming down the road. Each team had a rider smoking a cigarette. If it rained, everybody was on their own.

The marriage of mechanization and the internal combustion engine being new to the workings of war, considerable confusion existed as to how to put many of these wonders of industry to task. The motorcycle was a classic example, misunderstood and not always welcome by the conservative elements that dominate military establishments.

**RCE soldiers aboard a Douglas Model B with sidecar, Cavalry Barracks, Mons, Belgium 1919.**

Motorcycles, some with sidecars, made their appearance amongst the Battalion's transport, the number of horses allowed being reduced as the number of Triumphs increased. While many officers who rode them were enthusiastic about their new mounts, there were those who deplored the necessity for change such as this. But at least a motorcycle did not require to be fed, curried, and watered at the end of a long hard day, suffered no pain and when hit did not have to be put out of its misery.[1]

Although the motorcycle was quickly dismissed as an appropriate tool for the time-honoured cavalry charge, several attempts

**A Triumph and its brave rider pose between two Clyno-Vickers machine-gun combinations. Note the ammunition-belt boxes and spare wheel on the Clynos.**

were made to convert it into an economical form of armoured vehicle. The most notable of these permutations within the Canadian forces was the Clyno-Vickers. By attaching a sidecar-mounted, water-cooled, belt-fed .303 Vickers machine gun to this 1000 cc V-twin motorcycle, it was hoped that a gunner could blast away at the enemy while the rider guided the machine in and out of action. Difficulties soon arose, however, as the free swinging machine gun (the gunner's only handhold was the end grips on the gun) was impossible to fire with any accuracy while bouncing over rutted roads and fields, putting troops on both sides in peril. Reports of gunners shooting off their own front tires were not uncommon, even when at rest.[2]

Fortunately, it was in the non-combatant role that the motorcycle was to excel. Sidecar-equipped motorcycles were used as transport for officers and munitions, especially in England and Canada, while both sidecar and solo machines occasionally saw duty as tractors, pulling small-calibre artillery pieces to the front. And the motorcycle proved a natural for escort duty, where its advantage of speed and mobility reduced the burden of controlling troop and traffic movements. It permitted the rider quick access to potential trouble spots, even through the congestion of behind-the-lines troop and munitions movements:

> A Traffic Control man astride a motor-cycle escorted the Battalion from Dainville, through the tortuous, rubble heaped streets of Arras to the railway station . . .[3]
>
> 2nd Canadian Battalion marched 6 kms to nameless crossroads where a long line of motor-buses waited to bear them to their still unknown destination . . . Preceded by a motor-cyclist the convoy journeyed through the dark, moonless night . . .[4]

**The arm band just above this DR's right elbow signifies priority over all other traffic as he transports a wicker basket of pigeons toward the front.**

It was in the capacity of a message carrier that the motorcycle established itself as an indispensable fixture of the CEF. Communication was primarily the function of the Royal Canadian Corps of Signals (RCCS) which had not yet achieved autonomy from the Royal Canadian Engineers (RCE). There were sixteen riders in each division directly attached to the RCCS. Faced with the unreliable nature of early electrical communication systems, the RCCS used every means at its disposal to get messages through, as evidenced during the battle of Somme in 1916: "Pigeons, motorcyclists, runners, wireless, visual communication across the ground or relayed via balloons and spotting aeroplanes, all had their place in the scheme."[5]

Wireless radio technology was improving rapidly, along with the ability of the enemy to intercept transmissions. Interceptions were not a serious problem with the DR Letter Service. When radio security restrictions increased, as was the case during the advance from Amiens in 1918, use of DRs increased correspondingly.

Signal linemen used motorcycles to patrol telephone and radio lines for breaks. DRs with large wicker baskets strapped to their backs transported over one hundred carrier pigeons every day to battalions and batteries waiting in the trenches (although by 1915 the birds had begun to lose favour over the alternatives; the handling of pigeons became a problem without sufficient numbers of "pigeoneers" to look after them). Less frequently, wireless sets were transported to observation points in sidecars, but "wireless units could not yet be readily transported without damage to internal electrics."[6]

Turn-of-the-century mechanical devices, while steadily improving, were still cursed with questionable reliability. A motorcyclist had to be familiar with a host of adjustments and simple repairs. Each DR was supposed to receive instruction in the following:

> (I) Identify the parts of the motor cycle. (II) Lubricating. (III) Repairing and replacing tires. (IV) Adjusting brakes. (V) Driving-chains. (VI) Bearings. (VII) Adjusting belts. (VIII) Adjusting magneto. (IX) Adjusting carburettor. (X) Management of acetylene lamps. (XI) Manipulation of gas and air levers. (XII) Theory of petrol engine (though only qualified mechanics may repair the engine).
>
> If mechanical trouble is experienced when a motor cyclist is carrying a message, he has to decide whether time can be best saved by proceeding on foot, repairing the damage, or borrowing some other means of locomotion.[7]

Pre-war riders were usually young professionals as the motorcycle had not yet attained a mass appeal. They rode for the excitement of it, and not surprisingly, many of them answered the call for DRs when war broke out. During training, it was common practice to take these new recruits out for a group ride on their motorcycles. At a predetermined location, the riders were ordered to leave their machines and go for a rest in the woods. Sometime later, the sergeant major would order them back to the motorcycles and say something like, "Okay, let's go home for supper." Unfortunately, only the bikes of the officers and mechanics would start and these lucky riders deserted the rest, heading back to camp. The remaining group soon discovered that while they were off in the woods having a nap, the mechanics had disabled their bikes. The only way back was to find the fault and fix it. Late arrivals for dinner were the rule, rather than the exception.

An aspect of DR training, and one that all the First World War soldiers were subject to, was the "bacteriological tests," best defined in the words of a War Office memo. On 15 January 1919 authority was granted for the formation of a Signal Detachment at Kinmel Park Camp, the detachment comprising of two DRs and five cycle orderlies, with the following proviso: "They will be accompanied by all Regt Documents and a medical certificate showing freedom from all infectious diseases, skin diseases, and vermin. They will carry the unused portion of the day's rations."

The First World War rider's uniform consisted of a high-collared, hip-length service tunic, matching breeches or jodhpurs with suspenders, a sheep-skin overcoat or three-quarter length wool overcoat, dust goggles with a field service cap or British-style metal combat helmet for headgear, ankle-length army boots with leather leggings, and black leather gauntlet-style gloves. Under the coat was a Sam Brown belt with an Enfield M1 .38.

The famous winged-wheel DR badge was worn on the left sleeve just below the elbow. While the Signal Corps wore a blue and white band on the right arm, the DRs displayed the band on the upper-left sleeve or sometimes on both sleeves.

Louvred goggles were issued for travel in rain and snow. The rider peered through slits and by all accounts, the system worked, likely a factor of the low speeds a wise rider adhered to when out in foul weather. For cold weather riding, handlebar muffs were sometimes made available.

**An 11th Field Ambulance Corps DR shows off a typical WWI uniform. The leather strap around the front forks of the motorcycle increased front end rigidity. The toolbox and inner tube attached to the rear carrier were common accessories.**

**Parts supply problems prevented many Indians from accompanying Canadian troops to France.**

The most common motorcycles used by the CEF were the Indian, Triumph, and Clyno-Vickers. A limited number of Douglas machines were also used.

Initially, the CEF made much use of the Indian V-twins. It was thought their superior power would outweigh the disadvantages of importing the bikes first from the United States into Canada, and from there to Great Britain. The bureaucratic entanglement that followed this decision was typical of government at its worst—nothing gets done except the interdepartmental memos and even that takes time.

From the beginning, getting replacement parts for the Indians became a nightmare. Request after request for parts went either unfilled or only partially filled. Artificers tried desperately to maintain a DR service by cannibalizing worn-out bikes for replacement pieces. The Canadian camp at Shorncliffe noted that it had "three machines under repairs at all times." Fewer and fewer motorcycles became available for duty. Some units were told that the Indians assigned to them were "to be used only in case of emergency." No doubt this parts problem had a decided influence on the 4th Canadian Division's conclusion of 25 July 1916 that Indian motorcycles had not "proved suitable under general service conditions" and "Military Authorities Overseas are very much averse to Indian motor cycles being used with the Expeditionary Force."

Part of the blame for this mess lay with the constant government bungling. For instance, on 5 October 1916 a Canadian Signal Training depot in England ordered twenty-four different parts for a total of seventy-eight pieces. The order did not reach the Principal Ordnance Officer's desk in Ottawa, Canada, until 21 September 1935!

There is evidence, however, that the bulk of the delay may have been the result of a deliberate attempt by the British War Office to compel the CEF to buy British motorcycles in lieu of the "unserviceable" Indians. An 11 May 1916 letter from the Hendee Manufacturing Co. office in London, England, to Motor Transport Stores, Royal Canadian Army Service Corps (RCASC), at Shorncliffe alludes to the problem:

> In reference to your esteemed orders for parts, many of the parts are out of stock on account of the prohibition of imports, and upon receipt of the orders we immediately apply for license to import the goods, but up to the present no licences have been granted.
>
> One of our representatives was told today that the War Office stated that all together there were not more than eight Indian motorcycles in service. Now we certainly know this to be absolutely wrong, and we will appreciate it very much indeed if you will advise us to the best of your ability how many Indians there are in use amongst the Canadians, both in this country and at the Front.
>
> It is our constant desire, and that of our principals in Toronto to render the Canadian Contingent every service possible, but there seems to be some undercurrent trying to hamper us. PS: In reference to the sidecars which you have ordered, these are being made in this country and there will be no trouble in getting them through in a very short time.

The day after this was written, internal CEF correspondence showed that there were eighty-two Indian motorcycles at Shorncliffe alone. By 19 July 1917 the seriousness of the parts problem had caused the OC, Motor Transport, London area, to report that "it is now impossible to obtain any further supplies of spare parts for Indians in England" as they were all backordered to Canada.

Despite the problems, the ingenuity of unit mechanics somehow kept Indians and Canadian DRs on the road in England. A 29 August 1917 CEF letter stated that 104 solo and 54 combination Indians were being operated by Canadians at that time. Some relief came on 9 September 1917 when 70 percent of a parts order dated April of that year was shipped from Montreal ("14 cases motorcycles parts"), arriving in England 31 October. But this was certainly not enough to allow full use of the available machines.

What influence the alleged conspiracy had upon Canada's decision to buy Triumphs and Clyno-Vickers will never be known. Some English machines were purchased before the problem of Indian parts shortages erupted. Records show that as early as 7 June 1915 the Canadian Signal Troop in Canterbury received three Triumph motorcycles (frame nos. 263693, 263705, 263767) at £57.15.0 each (approximately $280 Cdn. at the then current exchange rates). There is no doubt that the single-cylinder Triumphs were well liked by the DRs, acquiring the nickname "Trusty Triumph" (admittedly, this word association also owed a great deal to the fact that Triumph's pre-war cable address was Trusty, Coventry).

In a letter from a captain in 2nd Canadian Division to Canadian Administration, dated perchance 11 November 1918, the author relates this personal tale of woe: "My motor bicycle is a Triumph. It has been evacuated to the base with a broken frame and I am awaiting a replacement. I consider it essential to the efficiency of my work to secure a Triumph in exchange." It is not stated why some other brand would have rendered his job inefficient, nor do we know if the request met with success.

Triumphs became the principal machine for Canadians on the European front. Triumphs were decidedly lighter and more manoeuvrable than Hendee Indians, which were used primarily in Canada and Britain, with some limited European exposure (e.g., at Flanders).

Even with soldiers' lives and the outcome of the war at risk, governmental bureaucracy continued to create problems. Lieutenant-Colonel McRae, Director of Supplies and Transport (S&T), Canadian Training Division, Sandgate, Kent, telegraphed his superiors on 14 March 1915 to request 9 solo motorcycles, 6 motorcycles with sidecars for guns, and 12 with sidecars for men and ammunition and 5 with box bodies, all for a squadron of 60 soldiers from the Eaton Machine Gun Brigade waiting to proceed overseas. The telegram was not even acknowledged until 8 January 1916.

As part of the continuing correspondence, Colonel McRae, in a letter to Major-General Carson dated 21 January, wrote the following jibe while clarifying a misconception concerning the requested equipment: "I quite appreciate that you would misunderstand; in fact it was a surprise to me to think that after all the money put in the Eaton 'armoured cars' they should proceed overseas with 'bicycles'."

On 15 July, a note to HQ from the War Office regarding "mechanical transport vehicles and motorcycles to complete the equipment of the 4th Canadian Division," listed 37 solo motorcycles, 3 motorcycles with sidecars, 5 motorcycles with sidecars for guns, and 12 motorcycles with sidecars for ammunition would be available at Kempton Park, Sunbury, Middlesex on 17 July. It went on to explain that the box body motorcars, motor lorries, and workshop and store lorries required were not available. Then on the seventeenth, the War Office phoned to say that they "regret that the following equipment only will be available" to be drawn 18 July: 1 motorcycle with sidecar, 5 motorcycles with sidecars for guns, and 6 motorcycles with sidecars for ammunition. How could 45 motorcycles vanish in two days?

On 3 November 1916 Divisional Signal Company requested 3 motorcycles: 2 for DR service and 1 light motorcycle for the OC's use in the course of his duties; and a kit of tools "for the use of an artificer who has been retained to look after minor repairs to motorcycles." The request was followed up on 6 December. "Up to date I have only received an answer concerning the kit of tools, which was refused me. I did not ask for a travelling repair workshop as some recent correspondence would suggest but for sufficient tools to carry out repairs a little beyond the sphere of a spanner and wrench." The OC further explains that "as I have before pointed out, 10 motorcycles were left in my charge to carry on what 22 machines had hitherto been doing," and without a motorcycle for personal transport, he had no means of reaching the "distant points of the Shorncliffe Command."

His answer came seven days later from the OC, RCASC Base Depot in which the subject of the requested motorcycles was passed over to someone else's desk at HQ, London. In reference to the tools, "it is not recommended that the Engineers make other than ordinary running adjustments. These should be effected with the tools supplied with each machine."

In 1916, the British Ministry of Munitions banned all production of motorcycles and automobiles for civilian use "for the duration." Realizing that few individuals had the money to purchase new machines anyway, it is likely this action was taken to serve mainly as a publicity gesture toward alleviating the problem of supply.

Not every attempt to obtain the elusive motorcycle met with failure. Previously refused by the British government because of the costs "and if any were issued to me all the other companies would ask for them," Lt-Col G. T. Denison, OC 2nd Division Cyclist Company, Dibgate Camp, Shorncliffe, took his request right to the top. Writing directly to Maj-Gen S. Hughes, Minister of Militia and Defence, on 12 August 1915, he asked that "a few motor cycles, to supplement the bicycles" be issued so that "the work would be more satisfactorily carried out. Would not the Canadian Government issue three or four to me." Hughes' office replied that "there will be four in stock in a few days now. They left Canada on the 2nd Aug."

Regardless of brand or country of origin, there were times in the field when parts simply could not get through. It then fell upon the DR or his unit's mechanic to keep the motorcycle operational. That they were able to succeed in so many cases is a credit to their inventiveness. Yet many of the improvised modifications were prompted not by necessity but by a desire to improve the machines. As previously mentioned, the first of crude foot-operated gear changers and twist grip throttle controls evolved out of this environment. There is also evidence that DRs from both sides arranged clandestine meetings in no-man's-land to swap superior British tires for the equally superior Bosch magnetos.[8] But the precedent for this parts exchange had been set early in the war by the motorcycle manufacturers themselves. Triumph, for example, shipped tires to neutral Holland, and in turn received, through Holland, Bosch magnetos. As trading with the enemy is not an approved practice in time of war, the Bosch connection was soon replaced with American Spildorfs and Dixies and the British ML.

It is impossible to estimate the quantity of motorcycles involved in the Canadian effort. Purchases were sporadic and from numerous sources, the transactions buried in mounds of paperwork now lost in time. Adding to the census confusion were the numerous privately owned motorcycles used on military business. At the onset of war, this practice was encouraged owing to the shortage of equipment available from the manufacturers. Many privately owned machines were pressed into duty, and the owners rarely received fair compensation, if any at all. Compensation also became a sore point for many riders who used their own motorcycles in the course of duty.

On 12 November 1915 three NCOs who had been using their personal machines requested reimbursement for mileage. One of them, A-Sgt E. C. Newall, had ridden 1,298 miles up to October of that year, and submitted a bill for $38.94, or three cents per mile. The official answer to his request was that the War Office did "not look with favour on granting mileage to DRs."

In some cases, DRs were compensated for supplying their own transportation, although the War Office repeatedly tried to put an end to the practice. A report dated 25 January 1916, recommended that the Canadian government "supply all necessary motorcycles and that use of hired motorcycles be discontinued as annual rental per machine equals $270, or roughly cost of motorcycles bought on open market."

The Department of Divisional Signal Company, ADMS Canadian, was ordered on 11 March 1916 to dispense with two privately owned motorcycles they were using, as Motor Transport "now have sufficient publicly owned motorcycles." The department's two makeshift DRs were replaced by one official DR from Shorncliffe. Unfortunately, one DR was not enough to do the job of two, to which Motor Transport replied "regret not having been able to furnish you with 2 owing to a shortage of motorcycles(?), but it is hoped that 2 will be supplied in future, as stated." The unauthorized use of private machines continued.

The War Office's obstinate stand resulted in injustices all around, as illustrated in the case of unsettled repair bills for two Rudge-Whitworth motorcycles, LA 1188, owned by Pte N. B. Hobart Sinclair, and LO 3467, owned by Cpl L. E. Massey. Headquarters refused to "compensate for use of private motorcycles in military capacity," so the two DRs requested a grievance and were again refused payment, even though the army was the beneficiary of the machines' use. It was HQ's contention that such expenses, regardless of how incurred, were the responsibility of the owners. Massey and Sinclair did not agree. On 20 March 1917 they went to France as reinforcements to the Heavy Artillery, leaving their unpaid bills behind with the owner of the repair shop.

Attitudes toward motorcycles have always been mixed, and even though their value in time of war had already been proven, factions opposed to their use never missed an opportunity to question the machines' effectiveness. Such an attack came in a 9 January 1917 letter from Canadian Administrative HQ (Quartermaster-General Department) to the Department of S&T suggesting DRs become Despatch Couriers, forsaking their motorcycles for the commuter train: "I am of the opinion that this is ever so much cheaper than at present, besides if the man was travelling by the same train each day we would then be sure of regular service uninterrupted by accidents, etc."

This letter, burdened with numerous mistakes in spelling and logic, went on to suggest buying season tickets to save even more. A highly dubious report was attached detailing the estimated costs of operating five motorcycles for three months, the figures exceeding the initial purchase cost of the machines by approximately 64 percent!

Coincidentally, on 8 May 1917 a letter to the quartermaster's office from General Staff, Canadians, showed that the estimated expenses for a one-week period to send despatches by post instead of DR would be $518, or about $330 more for the same hypothetical one-week period than the highly inflated estimates of motorcycle delivery costs offered by the QM's office in January.

The actual costs of motorcycle operation had already been established in a report dated November 1915, outlining a unit's official DR mileage for the month. Ten motorcycles rolled up 7,208 miles for a total expense of $219, or three cents per mile.

A few of those in charge, while not necessarily bubbling with open praise, at least recognized the motorcycle's value and advantages in carrying out certain functions. On New Year's Day 1916, a letter to the Secretary, HQ Canadian Overseas Military Forces, London, from Brigadier-General Meighen, OC Canadian Training Division, Bramshott, stated, "In view of the serious delay that has occurred recently in the postal delivery of important documents urgently required by your HQ, would it not be advisable to establish a DR Service between these and the London HQ?" By 1918, all Signal sections were getting DRs placed on their establishment.

Of course, any machine that possesses the attributes of speed and mobility is likely to tempt its operator to run afoul of the authorities. The 30 November 1916 record for the Metropolitan Police of London showed that a Cpl Leon K. Wiseman of the RCASC was stopped on the Victoria Embankment "for exceeding the speed limit of 20 mph." Later correspondence within CEF dated 6 December 1916 from J. Stavers, Staff Captain for Director of S&T, to QM General regarding Wiseman's speeding charge requested that the QM "report to this office as to the circumstances under which this non-commissioned officer (NCO) exceeded the speed limit on the date in question, when the matter will be taken up with the police with a view to having the summons cancelled."

In nearly every area of the world that witnessed the presence of Canadian soldiers during the First World War, Canadian riders were there on their motorcycles. Canada,

**Soldiers of the Canadian Scottish struggle to get a Clyno-Vickers through the mud.**

England, France, Belgium, Germany—even Russia—saw Canadian DRs when on 26 October 1918 the 16th Field Company, RCE, and the 6th Signal Company, RCE plus B Squadron of the Royal Northwest Mounted Police arrived in Vladivostok, Siberia. The Signal Company established a DR service in November, lasting right through a bitter winter until the force's departure in April of 1919.

Conditions on the European front were deplorable. During the battle for Passchendaele in October of 1917,

> the ground, in general, was super-saturated. There was greasy mud everywhere, even on the higher land from which the water would normally have run easily. Shell holes, in places lip to lip, were filled to the brim with water on the better ground, and in the lowest spots with noxious liquid mud. A few places in the forward areas had become swamp and quagmire, being almost impassable even on foot . . . the DRs had a thin time of it with the greasy mud.[9]

The DRs did have the advantage of being able to walk their machines through mud and ice, but sometimes even this was not enough to keep them going. Heavy mud often prevented the RCASC from getting through with gasoline supplies, which limited motor transport to trips of about thirty miles from an operating railhead.

It was under conditions such as this that Ernie Mount of Canadian Engineering, HQ staff, was awarded the Distinguished Conduct Medal with the following citation:

> This man carried urgent operation despatches to one of the assaulting divisions, the headquarters of which was continually on the move. After six hours search, over shell-torn and congested roads, and despite continuous

hostile fire, the concussion from which twice lifted him from his machine, severely injuring him, he finally delivered his despatches and brought back situation reports. His work undoubtedly assisted in the success of the operations.

Mount, along with many of his fellow DRs, received another injury too, a scar on his forehead, the result of running into telephone wire strung about four feet high across a road by the enemy. The wire was impossible to see at night, even with the bike's acetylene lamp lit.

Although it was popular to portray a daring DR speeding along with his head tucked down close to the fuel tank, experienced riders of the First World War tended to ride erect, watching for signs of the enemy. On frequently travelled routes, the rider knew which corners he would likely be fired upon, and noted the intervals between falling shells, adjusting his speed accordingly.

Competing with motorcycles for glamour in a young man's eyes were the new aeroplanes, and some DRs requested a transfer to pilot these flying machines. Yet planes were also becoming the DRs' hidden enemy. Unable to hear the approach of a plane because of the noise of a bike's engine, DRs on both sides of the conflict were often the targets of eager pilots. Harold Walton of the 159 Battalion, Algonquin Regiment, narrowly missed being hit by enemy aircraft fire as he crossed a bridge as it blew up behind him, knocking him and his bike down. As the enemy plane circled overhead, Walton lay in the mud playing dead. The ruse worked, the enemy flew away, and Walton delivered his despatch. Even when parked, motorcycles were often fired upon by aircraft, so it was not unusual for DRs to cover their machines with straw when the enemy was known to be patrolling the area skies.

**From left, Reg, Fritz, Percy, Ernie Mount, Chuck, Brownie, Sex and Jerry: the Canadian Engineers HQ DRs aboard Triumphs.**

**A DR races his Douglas through the battle zone.**

**Canadians enter Mons, Belgium, at the end of the First World War. The front of the Triumph ridden by the saluting soldier boasts an inner tube wrapped around its headlamp and a fender gone missing in action.**

In the drive to Cambrai, and then on to Valenciennes and Mons during October and November of 1918, "the DR Letter Service distinguished itself during this period. Its men moved mainly over crowded roads and sometimes through heavy shellfire looking for addresses whose locations were ever changing. As the availability of telephone service decreased, their work could only increase After the fighting at Valenciennes on the 1st and 2nd of November, the rate of advance caused the telephone service to become even more attenuated. The work of the DRs increased by leaps and bounds but relief was not long delayed.[10]

That relief came on 11 November 1918 when the enemy surrendered. Perhaps significant of the two-wheeler's importance to the war effort, the first Allied soldier to touch German soil after truce was declared did so upon a motorcycle.

# CPL BERT BENNES

3rd Signals Division, RCE

Bert Bennes attempted to join the CEF in 1914, "but they turned me down because I was underweight and wasn't healthy enough to take into the armed forces." At the time, Bennes worked for the city of Toronto in its purchasing department. "I used to have to go out every morning to see the foremen on the road and get the requisitions for material. I rode an Indian motorcycle." Previously, he had been a telegraph operator for the CPR, and it was using these latter skills that he was eventually able to sell himself to the army in January of 1916.

"I enlisted as a telegraph operator. There wasn't any schooling to do as I was already okay for it." By the end of May, Bennes was stepping off a boat in Liverpool, England, headed for Salisbury Plain. It was here that his telegraph career suffered a short circuit.

"The orderly officer and the sergeant walked by, looking you up and down to see if your boots were shining and so on. He had gone about eight or nine men past me when he came back and said, 'I know you.'

I said, 'I don't know you.'

He said, 'Where are you from?'

'From Toronto.'

'What do you do there?'

'I work for the city of Toronto.'

'You ride a motorcycle.'

'Yes.'

**Above: Cpl Bert Bennes, 18 June 1918 at Brule, France. The throttle and gearshift on his Triumph have been modified to operate by foot. Like Bennes, many DRs wore twin arm bands for quicker recognition among troops.**

'You're a despatch rider, not a telegraph operator.'

'I'm a telegraph operator.'

'You're in the army and you'll do as you're damn well told.'

"From then on I was a DR. They didn't need to teach me anything, for heaven's sake. I'd been riding a motorcycle every day for two or three years in Toronto."

Bennes started his DR career riding Indians. A training expedition took several neophyte DRs over to Abbeville, France, "to see if we could ride. That's when we found out that the Indians and Harley-Davidsons were just no damn good. You couldn't keep them on the road."

In fairness, the problem had more to do with the roads of France than the motorcycles. The roads were built of *pavé,* a high-crowned surface of cobblestone. When it rained, traction was minimal. And the heavier the bike, the more severe the problem. "The Indian and Harley-Davidson were too heavy. I don't know how many tumbles I took, especially in the dark. Geez, I still got a sore knee from it." No doubt the Canadian DRs expressed considerable relief when the CEF in France began using the lighter, more tractable Triumphs.

From Abbeville, DRs were assigned to various divisional Signal HQs when reinforcements were needed. Bennes went to 3rd Division Signals.

"You get a despatch, operation orders that had to go from CEF HQ, come up to army, from army to corps, from corps to division and so on. They tried to use the telephone. They had cable wagons carrying a drum of cable, pulled by six horses. The cable only lasted until the first scrap and then it's all blown up. We used to take the orders from division to brigade. We never went beyond Brigade HQ except when there was a scrap on. Then we went forward as far as we could safely go.

"About twenty-five days out of the month, we were riding on good roads with no shell fire except at crossroads. Every five minutes, the enemy would shell a crossroad. We'd stand back and wait until the shell came and then go like hell down the road."

The barrels of the big guns got extremely hot, needing about five minutes to cool down between firings.

Night riding without lighting was always dangerous, but compounding the danger was the enemy's use of flares. "I was going down the road one night when a flare dropped. The night just lit up like daylight. Well, I knew where there was a dugout. I was going just as fast as I could when I jumped off the motorcycle. It went flying into the barbed wire and I went down into the dugout and the bombs came down on the road.

"One of the worst things I hit at night was the rear end of a mule. The night was blacker than the ace of spades and I went right in between the mule's legs. He just let go and I went flying into the mud, the motorcycle on top of me.

"A motorcycle wouldn't last two months. But DRs were the biggest bunch of thieves. Some officers had an inside track to the supply column. They were getting brand-new motorcycles even though they weren't entitled to them. If they left those motorcycles without a guard on them, we'd steal them. One time we heard that two officers were having a beer so four of us went to this town, two fellows on each machine. Casually, the two extra men hopped onto the officers' motorcycles and away they went back to HQ. We worked all night dismantling those motorcycles.

"One fellow needed a rear wheel, one fellow the handlebars, another a front wheel, another a gearbox. The next day there was a message, 'Two motorcycles stolen from such and such a place' with the numbers. But we'd file the numbers off, throw our bashed up pieces into the canal and have new parts. That's the way we kept the motorcycles going."

Officers' motorcycles were favourite targets for enterprising DRs in need of parts.

The battle for Vimy Ridge was an important one for Canada, a nation then a mere fifty years old. All previous attempts to capture the ridge by other Allied troops had failed. For the first time, 9 April 1917, the four divisions of the Canadian Corps were united into one fighting force. At dawn, on Easter Monday, the Canadians attacked the ridge in the midst of a driving blizzard. By mid-afternoon, the Canadians had overrun the entire ridge with the exception of two small pockets. Three days later, these, too, were in Canadian hands.

"During Vimy, I was in reserve. We were two or three miles to the rear running despatches. The area was devastated. When I got word that the Canadians had taken Vimy, I was on my motorcycle. We didn't find out for two or three days. There was this bombardment going on, the guns wheel-to-wheel. It was just hell popping over. I didn't know what was going on, I just knew that I had a despatch to take from here to there and get back as quick as I can.

"About a week or so after, I was going along the top of Vimy Ridge at night. The enemy was just down the hill and it was pitch black. The only way you could tell you were on the road was to drag your feet. You could feel the cobblestones. I was going pretty slow when, well dammit, in front of me there were sparks all along the road!"

When Bennes returned to HQ and related this strange occurrence to the others, he was told what the sparks were—machine-gun bullets. "If I would have sped up, I would have run into them."

At the bottom of the ridge were duckboards, a path of wooden slats laid over the mud. "Well you try and ride those on a wet night. I was riding out onto the duckboards when a shell landed that wasn't ten feet from me. It went into the mud which just came up like a shower, then I went off into the mud. I picked that motorcycle up out of the mud with both hands and put it back onto the duckboards. To this day, I don't know how I did it.

"We worked on the motorcycles every day. I was down the road one time and there was a heck of a racket from the engine. It wouldn't go. So I took the head off to find the skirt on the piston had broken. I broke off what was left, put the head back on and rode back to camp. It took me half an hour to do that, but geez, I would have had to walk twenty miles.

"We always carried a map of the area that we were in. It showed us the roads and the bridges. You know that old saying never cross a bridge before you come to it? But be damned sure the bridge is there when you do come to it. Many a time the bridge was there when we went by, but it wasn't on the way back."

It was common knowledge that a DR always had a map, so they were often called upon for directions by other Allied troops. On one occasion, Bennes came to meet the Prince of Wales as a result. "He was a drunken bum you know, stationed at Canadian Corps HQ. He and another guy were riding horseback and had crossed a split in the road. They didn't know which road to take so they stopped me and wanted to have a look at my map.

"The last hundred days of the war, going down to Roisel from Arras, the enemy was on both sides of the road. We didn't know whether they were going to fight or give up. Well, I went down that road and I'm telling you, you couldn't see me for dust!"

The enemy did give up, and on 11 November 1918 the war was over. "We had one man killed in the two and a half years I was with 3rd Division Signals. He slid under a truck one night. The rest of them were broken bones—arms and legs—and three of them went for air pilots. I went in as a junior man and came out as a sergeant of the section, although it doesn't say so in the paybooks. That was because I didn't want it to."

As a means of encouraging people to volunteer for the CEF, the city of Toronto agreed to supplement the pay of any employee who joined the army, bringing up the wages received as a serviceman to that received prior to enlisting. Bennes was entitled to $7.30 a week from the city, which was sent to his mother. Had his pay increased as a result of a promotion, the city would have reduced its portion to reflect the change. Bennes preferred that his mother got the money so he declined all promotions.

He did, however, receive a Military Medal. "I don't know what I got it for. It just came in the mail."

Bennes returned to his mother and job in Toronto 10 March 1919.[11]

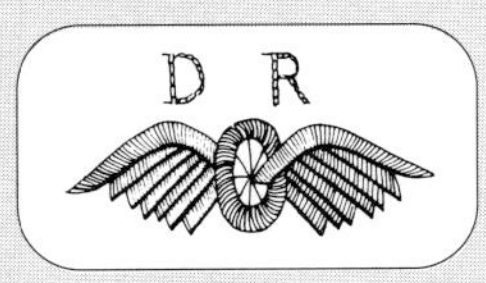

# BETWEEN WORLD WARS

The end of the war did not mark an immediate return home for Canadian troops. The process of getting such a large body of soldiers back to Canada was a slow one, and some stayed on as part of the Army of Occupation in Germany. Yet by the time the Treaty of Versailles was signed on 28 June 1919, putting an official end to the hostilities, very few Canadians remained in the armed forces, at home or abroad.

*—By Pte. Stewart Cameron*
Saturday Night Bath

The First World War, the Great War, was supposed to be the war to end all wars. Too many people had suffered. It was a time to forget and start anew. To disarm. A government now nearly 450 percent deeper in debt than it had been at the outbreak of war had no money to spend on a peace-time army. The degree of universal uninterest was such that few records of between-the-wars activity survived. The military of the time was largely made up of volunteer militia, mostly self-financed and self-equipped.

Canada's Permanent Force in 1921 numbered a mere 4,125, a figure that would not be exceeded during the next five years. In 1923, morale reached a low point when a show of Canada's military might saw just over 2,000 men turn out for a major exercise that lasted only four days. That same year, the RCCS began to man the radio-telegraph stations of the Northwest

Territories and Yukon Radio System. During the Depression of the 1930s, Canada's military was placed in charge of the Unemployment Relief Camps and related work projects. By the mid 1930s, events in Europe once again threatened war and the Canadian government slowly eased spending restraints.

In 1936, a dishevelled and disheartened militia was reorganized into the Non-Permanent Active Militia (NPAM) and thus began a program of modest improvement. That same year, the Canadian Signal Training Centre in Barriefield, Ontario, was established. This centre would prove to be an important base for training army motorcyclists.

In 1939, the Permanent Force received its first new uniforms since the First World War, and another first, army issue boots. That same year, summer camp for the Algonquin Regiment in northern Ontario saw 250 NPAM volunteers turn up in old uniforms to be trained in First World War tactics.

Motorcycles fell into begrudging favour among the military during this period of fiscal neglect because, compared to the preferred armoured vehicles, motorcycles were inexpensive to purchase and operate. Consequently, these diminutive machines found use not so much in their traditional roles of convoy duty and message delivery, but as substitutes for the heavy armour of trucks and tanks in militia exercises and manoeuvres. Canada had no tanks, anti-aircraft guns, armoured cars or armoured machine-gun carriers until 1938, yet motorcycles could be found in virtually every unit of reasonable size or importance.

The number of motorcycles was small, yet their presence was disproportionately high when compared to the more expensive machines of war. Much variety in brand was evident, with appearances being made by BSAs, Hendee Indians, Harley-Davidsons, Nortons, and Scotts.

Use of privately owned vehicles was encouraged, although rarely compensated for, which added to the menagerie of makes. Those who turned out for training between the wars were at the very least dedicated, for neither their government nor fellow countrymen showed much interest.

A comprehensive Canadian Army Training Pamphlet for motorcyclists was issued in 1932 with the following proviso: "The lessons contained herein are based on the light type of motorcycle. If the machines provided are of the heavy type, ie, Harley-Davidson, Indian, etc, some minor departures from the text will be necessary."[12]

A later warning brings to the attention of instructors a riding habit peculiar to Canadian military motorcyclists and one decidedly frowned upon by their commanding officers: riding upon the tank. The origins of, and reason for, this bizarre practice remain a mystery.

> During instruction on motorcycles any tendency on the part of the candidates to become over-confident must be watched and suppressed. Over-confidence allied with a desire to "show-off" may tend to make them adopt bad habits, such as riding on the fuel tank and other such tricks.[13]

The motorcycle training course lasted four weeks. Each student was theoretically issued with a crash helmet, protective clothing and rubber boots, although in practice the equipment was rarely available.

Training covered basic riding skills, riding over "sandy banks, fords, narrow bridges, bogs and rocky paths." It also included such tasks as "riding on the left side of the road, moving in formation, taking cover, riding machines to earth and opening fire, riding with respirators, manhandling machines, travelling through smoke, riding in ditches, etc." Students were taught how to "bail out with least damage to man and machine. This

**The RCCS detachment at Camp Petawawa in 1934 included these two Scott two-stroke motorcycles.**

is a drill to be learnt but not to be practised except in an emergency." Courses related to DR work included "map reading, knotting and lashing, jointings—field cable, telephone and use of soldering outfit."

Yet even with these intense four weeks behind him, "the motorcyclist must not be considered as fully trained immediately after he has completed a course and qualified as a motorcyclist. It is experience and experience alone that makes a motorcyclist a useful man."[14] Getting that experience was not easy with so little equipment available, which probably explains why the bulk of the course and training covered maintenance.

In 1934, a RCCS detachment in Petawawa, Ontario, made use of liquid-cooled, two-stroke Scotts, although this type of engine was rarely seen in British and Canadian forces because of a mutual Defence Department preference for the typically more reliable four-strokes. In another radical departure from tradition, during a general mess meeting that same year at Petawawa, the decision was made to let all subscriptions to horse magazines end, and to replace them with "some suitable motor magazine."[15]

A sidecar-equipped 1,200 cc Harley-Davidson Model V was used for manoeuvres by many armoured outfits, such as the Carden Loyd Carrier Machine Gun Platoon,[16] Royal Canadian Regiment based in London, Ontario. Because of its excessive weight, the bike was usually ordered with an optional reverse gear.

**PPCLI DRs ready for royal escort duty. Two 1938 Triumph Speed Twins stand before a row of Triumph Tigers.**

For the May 1939 visit to Canada by King George VI and Queen Elizabeth, Triumph Speed Twins and Tigers were purchased for use by the B Company, Princess Patricia's Canadian Light Infantry (PPCLI) when on escort duty for the royal couple.

As in the past, Canada's commitment and finances would not permit development of modern military equipment on its own, so again it chose to monitor the efforts of other countries like England.

By the 1930s, England's fear of global conflict was growing, and the British War Department reacted by developing a motorcycle specifically designed for the theoretical needs of war. From specifications born in committees unfamiliar with motorcycles sprang an overweight, mechanically complicated, expensive 500 cc V-twin manufactured by BSA, known appropriately as the model WO (War Office) or Model J12. It proved unpopular as a civilian motorcycle, and would prove to be an equally unwelcome mode of transport in the coming war. Very few got into Canadian hands; the 1st Field Company, RCE, stationed in Petawawa was the sole pre-war outfit on record to sample the bike's shortcomings.

**The 1st Field Company, RCE, and a BSA Model J12 on summer exercise at Petawawa, Ontario, in 1938.**

# THE SECOND WORLD WAR

From a historical point of view, it is easy to question the judgement of the non Axis-aligned nations leading up to the Second World War. That conflict was imminent now seems obvious, as does the fact that the Allies were decidedly caught with their armaments down. No Allied nation wanted war. No Allied nation was ready for it, perhaps least of all Canada. The Second World War began in 1939, initiated by Germany's invasion of Poland on 1 September. Two days later, Australia, Britain, France, India, Newfoundland[17] and New Zealand declared war on Germany. Canada waited another seven days before adding its name to that declaration.

On both sides of the conflict, motorcycles were to play an important role. Between September 1939 and May 1945, approximately seven hundred thousand motorcycles were produced for the combined Allied effort. These numbers are all the more impressive when one considers the unfavourable perception of motorcycling that has always plagued the machine in North America. The Canadian military, itself not completely immune to the perception, addressed the attitude problem in the Canadian Army Training Memorandum, No. 6, of 1941:

> In Canada, generally speaking, there appears to be an entirely erroneous conception of the present- day motorcycle. The general opinion exists that a motorcycle is merely a glorified bicycle for the younger generation. Any appreciation of the tremendous power built into these vehicles seems to be quite overlooked. Actually they are anything but a toy, and in the hands of an inexperienced rider are capable of causing serious loss of life and limb. If the proper perspective of the motorcycle situation can be instilled into the Canadian Military Forces, a great forward stride will have been made in attaining the standard of efficiency so imperative to modern warfare.

Motorcycles were an inexpensive and plentiful source of transport for Canada's growing army, as illustrated by this long row of Nortons issued to the 4th Princess Louise Dragoon Guards in Worthing, England, 7 January 1942.

The role of the military motorcycle during the Second World War was to remain primarily non-combatant, yet greatly expanded over its use in the First World War. The motorcycle would see action in daily despatch duties, reconnaissance, intelligence and provost duties, escorting convoys, traffic control, emergency parts and medical deliveries, carrying war correspondents' stories back to the censor, and emergency communications when the other systems failed. A DR was also required to report to the fire marshal's office whenever a fire alarm sounded. "In all of these activities the motorcycle, due to its mobility, speed and compactness, is irreplaceable."[18]

Recognition of these attributes resulted in riders from outfits like the 2nd Reconnaissance Squadron chasing the smoke trails of downed enemy aircraft in order to make an arrest before the survivors had an opportunity to escape. DRs in other outfits rushed to the scene of Allied air crashes with orders to extricate the survivors from the plane before it exploded.

Even the occasional padre or chaplin took advantage of this mobility to get to hospitals and "the odd crash that occurs in the neighbourhood."[19] Equipped with a sidecar, the motorcycle also became an efficient means of transporting officers.

Since the war of 1914-1918, communication technology had made impressive advances, yet it was still not deemed a dependable method of getting the message through. Telephone and telegraph lines often broke or were cut, while wireless radio proved unreliable. Messages by both means were easily intercepted. And homing pigeons were not the answer either: "These perverse birds all seemed to fly towards the German lines."[20] However, the speed and mobility of the motorcycle made it an excellent choice for message delivery, and riders almost universally took great pride in ensuring that the mail was delivered, even if the rider had to abandon his bike and crawl through mud under enemy fire.

A DR on a Harley-Davidson escorts a convoy of emergency food to the Netherlands, 3 May 1945.

As in the First World War, an attempt was made to use the motorcycle in a combatant role as an economical alternative to armoured transport. The Royal Canadian Dragoons, Lord Strathcona's Horse (Royal Canadians),

Governor General's Horse Guards, 17th Duke of York Royal Canadian Hussars, 8th (Princess Louise) New Brunswick Hussars and the British Columbia Dragoons were all designated as motorcycle regiments while stationed in Canada during the early stages of the war. When more money became available, all but the 17th Duke of York Royal Canadian Hussars were converted to armoured regiments, the former becoming the 7th Reconnaissance Regiment.

Canada had a scant fourteen tanks when war was declared. Initial recruits made do with improvised uniforms, rifles, and precious little ammunition or transport. The 17th Duke of York Royal Canadian Hussars, 3rd Motorcycle Regiment, received their first official shipment of motorcycles, two sidecar units, on 9 September 1940, almost one year to the day after Canada had declared war. Eight days later, another thirty-two machines arrived. By the end of the year, the regiment could boast of ninety-seven motorcycles in total.

**DR J.W. King accepts a pigeon-transported message from Corporal Hanley, 10 February 1943. The toolbox attached to the bike's front fender and the location of the horn (below the headlight) show that this is an early model (pre mid-1941) Harley-Davidson WLC.**

The 6th Fortress Signals Company, RCCS, stationed in Halifax, acquired an unexpected supply of motorcycles when France surrendered to Germany on 22 June 1940. The French luxury liner *Pasteur* had just sailed from the United States with a load of military equipment bound for France. When the ship stopped at Halifax harbour for the supplies, the crew of the HMCS *Andrée Dupré* boarded the ship and informed its captain of his country's new alliances. Faced with the option of surrendering or being blown out of the water, the captain chose to hand over his ship and cargo to the Allies. On board the *Pasteur* was a consignment of Indian Chief motorcycles outfitted with sidecars, crash bars and metric instruments. The 6th Fortress Signals received a half dozen of these liberated machines.

Similarly rigged Indians also ended up in the hands of a few Canadian outfits stationed in England, but rare finds such as this did little to relieve the paucity of equipment. Out of desperation, a normally conservative military establishment took whatever came its way. It was not unusual for volunteers to turn up for initial training on their own motorcycles, and continue to use these machines while in training. Others generously loaned their own machines to the army as a personal contribution to their country's war effort. The thanks they received was not always commensurate with the sacrifice they made.

In June of 1940, Frank Bastien of Montreal loaned his 1934 Brough Superior to the 17th Duke of York Royal Canadian Hussars, one month before the 3rd Motorcycle Regiment was mobilized. The machine was given a Department of National Defence (DND) number and used for training until 1943 when, unknown to Bastien, who had by then enlisted with the RCAF, the bike was condemned and withdrawn from service.

After the war, Bastien returned to Montreal to discover that his pride and joy had been scrapped. Following a mountain of bureaucratic paperwork, on 20 May 1947, Bastien was denied any compensation for the loss of his bike, worth about four hundred dollars then and near priceless now.

**No. 5 Provost Company in pre-war summer dress. The two motorcycles on the left are Indian Scouts. The two on the right are Indian Chiefs.**

Because of the unusual demands placed upon the rider, even recruits with considerable civilian motorcycle experience were required to participate in extensive training programs. The Canadian Army Training Memorandum, No. 6, claimed that the usefulness of a motorcycle was more dependent upon rider skill than was the case for "most other Army vehicles." It further stated "the motorcycle is perhaps the least understood and, for that reason, the most abused vehicle in military service." Because of this, training not only included a vigorous riding program but also an equally intense maintenance course. "The normal period of training a motorcyclist is two weeks, during which time 26 hours individual riding should be allowed for each man," the remaining time being allotted to such things as mechanical theory, maintenance, daily and weekly inspections (known as the Task System) and map reading.[21]

**2Lt W. Shenstone, Governor General's Horse Guards, riding his own 500 cc, OHV, BSA single, 30 September 1940.**

Aside from dealing with basic and advanced riding theory, as applied to both solo and sidecar, the course also touched on "How to Fall":

> When a machine gives the impression that it is about to go out of control the rider should allow full play to its natural stability by opening up the throttle and at the same time remaining as far as possible part of the machine. . . . There comes the time, however, when this proves impossible and the important thing is to fall off in such a manner that

> there is no damage either to the machine or the individual. To avoid damage to the rider is easy. What is a little more difficult is to insure that the machine is unharmed.[22]

Laying a motorcycle down, sometimes the most effective way of stopping a bike equipped with token brakes.

To minimize damage to the machine, instruction was given on how to lay a motorcycle down, the method of slowing a motorcycle by dropping it onto its side while it is in motion. This seemingly bizarre practice was an effective means of reducing speed in emergencies prior to the advent of useful brakes.

The most prominent Canadian centre of learning for military motorcyclists was at the Canadian Signal Training Centre at Barriefield near Kingston, Ontario. Capt Bernie Nicholson was placed in charge of the riding school in 1942, and a short time later was also given the responsibility of the mechanics' school. "Our initial challenge," said Nicholson, "was to reduce the high level of accidents, injuries and fatalities in motorcyclist training and service. Substantial progress was achieved quickly by improved instruction, identifying and eliminating bad riding habits, and the good influence of some very steady instructors."

Mornings were spent in the classrooms learning the fine points of map reading and motorcycle mechanics. Afternoons were spent on the bikes, riding on good roads, secondary roads, cross-country, through ditches and over hills. To get riders used to riding in total darkness, during night exercises the headlights were gradually taped over until only the regulation slit was left to light a trainee's way.

Norton 16Hs await student mechanics.

Games, like the mess tin hunt, were often played to lighten the load of learning. Each rider was given a map reference where his mess tin was located. Using only those co-ordinates, he rode out into the surrounding country in search of his next meal.

As in the First World War, appetite was also used as an incen-

**The mechanicals of this cutaway Harley-Davidson were operated by an electrically powered drum (built into the bench) which turned the rear wheel.**

tive for students to pay attention during the morning lessons in mechanics. When out in the field, instructors would sometimes sabotage the students' bikes. The stranded riders' ability to return to camp for dinner would then depend upon their ability to make the necessary repairs.

When Canadian troops arrived in England, the training continued. One battalion already stationed there published the following poem to commemorate the arduous nature of what lay in store for the newly arrived soldiers:

The Coys sent us raw recruits,
To train on cycles Norton,
But if they last the whole six days,
I'll treat you to a short 'un.

**DRs Doug Reid and Norman Given examine a map while on a training exercise in England, 19 May 1944. Note the winged wheel patch prominently displayed on the DR's left arm.**

## L-CPL RALPH YULL

RCCS

Ralph Yull had not the slightest suspicion that the Royal visit to London, Ontario, during May of 1939 would indirectly be responsible for his induction into Canada's armed forces. "Several of the riders who hung around Rae Watson's cycle shop were contacted by the London military headquarters and asked to form a group of outriders to escort the royal procession on tour through the city. We gladly agreed, for this would mean riding in close proximity to the King and Queen for a half hour or so. However, in order to wear the uniform, we had to join the militia (1st Company, Signals), which we did with the understanding that we would be discharged once the parade was over."

Most of the royal tour escort group failed to take their discharge. On 1 September 1939, this group was "invited, on a no-refusal basis, to appear at MO No. 1 HQ where we were exhorted to join the Signal Corps and see the world. Most of us signed up in the Canadian Active Service Force (CASF).

"We immediately moved into Wolseley Barracks and went under canvas. I escaped all fatigue and guard duties by using my own 1935 Indian 4 and sidecar (the prettiest machine I have ever ridden) to run DRLS and SDR to MD HQ in downtown London (at $3.50 per diem)."

The sidecar rig proved to be of great value for ferrying officers between camp and headquarters, and not all of that value was derived from the standpoint of transportation, at least for Yull. "I used to have this trick of swerving sharp right and then sharp left while leaning my machine, leaving the hapless passenger in a sidecar with the wheel well up in the air and him screaming for release!

Recruits trickled in and soon, on paper anyway, we had a DR Section, with thirty-two riders lined up. When George Sturman, who had raced bikes on cinder-tracks, appeared, it was pretty obvious who would become sergeant. The other NCO positions (corporal and lance corporal) were not filled, but it didn't matter a great deal for, at the time, we had no issue of motorcycles and wore First World War uniforms. On the Indian, I wore my own high-cut boots, which in fact I also wore overseas in December 1939, aboard the last of the four funnel liners, *Aquitania*."

**Above: Early-pattern Nortons of the 1st Canadian Division Supply Company, RCASC, line an English country road during a training exercise in February 1941. Military Norton 16Hs manufactured from late 1942 on received some minor production changes, such as pannier racks and a small pillion seat in lieu of the rear carrier pictured here.**

Yull's unit arrived in Scotland on 19 December and then was moved by train to Aldershot, England. "Almost at once, our section was issued motorcycles, for in a couple of days we were to commence DR runs to CMHQ at 2 Cockspur St., Canada House, in Trafalgar Square." The ranks of the section had swollen to thirty-five by now, for which they received five motorcycles total to carry out their duties, "500 cc Nortons and BSAs. Snortin' Nortons and Beezas we called them.

"I had always ridden Indians, Harleys, and other American hand-shift machines, so I found it a bit of a change to ride a foot-shift, hand-clutch machine on the wrong side of an ice-and-snow-covered road (and with no nice supportive sidecar). I (now ascended to the dizzy heights of lance corporal) or Sergeant Sturman would take a neophyte in tow on the daily run to London, about forty-five miles one way.

"Soon, each man was issued his own machine and we then began months of training while continuing to carry on with DR runs between all units of 1st Canadian Division and HQ in London. There were rough riding sessions over any terrain, classes on map reading, motor mechanics, daily maintenance—our most enjoyable activity was the rough riding sessions. We would head out in file to Long Valley, with a NCO front and rear. Long Valley is a semi-wild heath with very broken ground, steep hills, narrow trails through rocks and bush, and quite often a large and very wet marshy area. We would plunge into the swamp to see who, if anyone, could get through, and then wander in to help the usual stick-in-the-mud.

"We also belted our poor little 500 cc side-valve Nortons up what looked to be impossibly steep hills, sometimes making it, sometimes rolling backward, which called for some frantic footwork. Those of us who had ridden American cycles pre-war and who, by and large, held a contempt for English machines, soon learned how far ahead English design and manufacture was to the low-slung, butt-dragging American designs. Later, when our Nortons were replaced with Harley 45s, we were quickly reminded of the difficulty of trying to extricate a massive, heavy Harley out of a ploughed field with its sump embedded firmly in the muck and the rear wheel spinning helplessly.

"We used to fabricate the necessity for map-reading tours, which were no more than joy rides, although some map-reading proficiency did result that no doubt paid off later. On one such occasion, I led a file of perhaps fifteen riders along country roads and ended up at Windsor Castle. We approached the gate guards and asked if we could enter to do a bit of touristing." The answer was no. However, Sir John Hanbury-Williams, who had a fondness for Canadians, happened to be passing by, heard the familiar accent of Yull and his friends, and promptly invited them in for a personally conducted tour of the castle. This included his own residence in the Round Tower, where he pointed out a painting of the Battle of Omdurman, the last battle fought by the British army in redcoats. Sir John had fought alongside Winston Churchill.

Yull and his group left the castle elated, and made their way to Weybridge, not far from the famed Brookland's race track. "For every red-blooded Canadian youth raised on *Chums* and *Boys Own Annual*, Brookland's was the race track of the world. Making our way to the side fence, we found the steeply banked track had, horrors, been interrupted with the construction of a factory building Vickers aircraft. Right across the track! Circumnavigation was impossible.

"By devious and nefarious means, we gained access to the part of the track still open. It resembled a giant soup bowl, with the outer rim rising perhaps thirty-five feet above the inner flat portion. My riders immediately went mad and freed themselves of any control I had been exercising to date, racing up and along the wall until the underpowered Nortons would no longer keep them in the Wall of Death position. I was worried, but went ahead and enjoyed myself, squeezing out the last sixty-eight miles per hour my Norton was capable of when one of my riders rode up all excited and alarmed. 'Pee Wee has gone over the edge!'

"We rode over to the point where Pee Wee's motorcycle had struck the high curb and flipped into the inner ring of the race track. All we could see were wild cucumber vines." After some searching, they found their comrade in a nest of alder shoots. He survived, but not without gaining a permanent limp. And Yull had some real talking to do. "No one seemed able to understand what in hell a training contingent of DRs was doing racing madly around Brookland's race track." Training to be Canadian DRs most likely.

**CTS instructor L-Cpl Walter Meldrum of the Royal Montreal Regiment illustrates the correct procedure for hill climbing at Boxhead Sandpit, Frensham Sands, near Bordon, Hampshire, England, 1 May 1942. The fire extinguisher attached to the right rear fender of his Norton was carried by instructors only. The DR students spectating are no doubt wondering what magic Meldrum weaves in order to coax a 13 hp 16H up such a steep incline.**

In early 1941, the Canadian Training School (CTS) was established at Bordon, Hampshire, England. Cpl George Hine, an instructor at the centre, recalls, "Personnel of all ranks from the 1st and 2nd Canadian divisions in England were trained in the use of the motorcycle. Officers were required to handle a bike for emergencies while ORs became DRs and convoy motorcyclists." Motorcycle training at the CTS continued well into 1943.

A variety of courses involving motorcycles were also offered at the School of Military Engineering, in Ripon, Yorkshire. A four-week course for NCOs included motorcycle riding, fault finding, assembly and route finding. Another taught officers as motorcycle instructors, and another offered instruction to would-be mechanics. One course, three weeks in duration and available only to qualified DRs, trained riders in motorcycle recovery in the field and repair by replacement of damaged parts from other machines. As an aside, the course for "push cycle repairers" was eight weeks long, twice that of any motorcycle course, which was a sad reflection on the continuing lack of CMHQ understanding of motorcycles.

By 1943, CMHQ's knowledge and appreciation of motorcycles had increased to the point that they were able to astutely observe that "there is a tremendous difference between driving a truck and riding a motorcycle."[23]

**Sergeant Hood of the Calgary Regiment reveals the mysterious inner workings of a Norton 16H engine to a CTS student.**

## SAPPERS GEORGE HODGSON AND LOU LAPOINTE

2nd Battalion, RCE

As George Hodgson recalls: "I just loved my DR'ing years. I rode with two great guys, Rod McGregor, a reinforcement rider to D Company, and Lou Lapointe, who, like myself, was an original member of D Company, 2nd Battalion, RCE."

D Company was a Prairie unit based in Winnipeg, Manitoba. The original members set sail for Britain 27 August 1940. Organized activities aboard the *M. V. Georgic* were designed to keep the lads out of trouble, and included such spectacles as obstacle races and boxing tournaments. The War Diary also mentions some less organized activities: "All officers and NCOs are responsible in seeing that no gambling occurs on board ship."

The company anchored at Gurrock, Scotland, 4 September, then immediately climbed aboard a train, arriving at Aldershot, Hampshire, a day later.

The company's first eight motorcycles were drawn from the Royal Canadian Ordinance Corps (RCOC) at 10 a.m., 30 September. At 4 p.m. the same day "CRE [Corps of Royal Engineers] advised adjutant no more m/cs available for indefinite period as manufacturers cannot fill orders." By 22 October six NCOs were listed as "duly examined and tested and have been found to have a thorough knowledge of, and sufficient skill to operate a m/c."

Hodgson: "On our last test, we had to take our bikes up to the LAD [Light Aid Detachment] at Southey Hall. The next morning, we were told by Billy Smith [corporal of DRs] that the LAD had done two or three things to our bikes. We had to find out what was wrong, fix the problem, then find Billy who would be waiting at a designated map

**Above: L-Cpl Tony Dziatkenich, Pte Cochrane, Sergeant Graham Alexander, DR Louis Lapointe and a rare untarnished Norton.**

reference point.

"I set my throttle, spark and air and went to kick the engine over. The kickstarter had been taken off its spline and turned in the down position, instead of being in the up position ready for kicking. I pulled it off and put it back in its proper position, gave the bike a couple of kicks and she roared to life. Half an hour later, roughly ten miles down the road, I found Bill, almost asleep lying in a ditch.

"As Bill had a list of what the LAD had done to the bikes, he asked me how come I had got to him so fast?" After explaining to the corporal what he had fixed, the corporal showed Hodgson what he had missed. Paper had been stuffed into the centre connector of the high-tension lead from the spark plug to the coil, which should have prevented the engine from firing. "If the bike hadn't started, I don't believe I would have checked the inside of the connector. I would probably still be trying to start the bike."

DRs learned to disconnect this same lead, pocketing it to deter theft whenever they had to leave their bikes.

> February 12, 1941. Found: Norton m/c with unit and serial number removed. Engine #W16953-79X100. [The W was Norton's code for the 16H engine, followed by the engine's number and then, after the dash, the measurements of the 500 cc single cylinder's bore and stroke.]
>
> March 30, 1941. Lost: Triumph m/c WDCC-74661, engine #3S.36541, reported stolen at Fetcham on night of March 15. [The 3S was Triumph's code for its 350 cc single cylinder.]
>
> April 11, 1941. DR to CRE returned empty-handed. First day on record.

With England experiencing its coldest winter in many years, riders were forced to develop unusual riding techniques to cope with the ice and snow. Lou Lapointe "used a new pair of rubber boots every day, as the only way you could keep the bike up straight was to drag your feet." The English winters wore on everything, from clothing to riders to the bikes.

Hodgson: "While stationed at a place called Dunsfold in Devon where the Battalion was constructing a fighter station for the RCAF, Rod, who had the oldest and most racked up bike of the three of us, got a call to report to the transport officer's hut with his bike. As DRs, we were able to see a lot of the country that the ordinary sappers never saw, and a lot of times we would go off the beaten path to where our work tickets really didn't allow us to go, so Rod thought he was going to catch hell for something or other he had pulled off."

At the time, D Company soldiers were billeted four to a small tent. Company DRs, however, were permitted the luxury of just two to a tent—and their motorcycles. "Where the two other guys would normally sleep, we would keep our machines to keep them out of that damp English climate. Anyway, Rod wheels his bike out, tickles the old Amal carburetor, kicks her over, and off he goes down to the transport office. An hour or so later, he returns on a brand-new Norton. He got off of it, pulled the bike back up on its stand, and of course he's sitting on the bike running her to see how she sounds and of course Lou and I are all around the bike, looking her over to see what's different from the old machine."

Eventually, Rod shut the bike down. Then Cpl Bill Smith came along to check out the new acquisition. Rod went to start it so he could hear the beauty run, but the beast refused to co-operate.

"He pressed down on the tickler, gave her a kick, she backfired, and the next thing we knew, the bike was on fire! There we were, four goofballs trying to put out the fire with our jerkins. We didn't succeed."

Rod's new pride and joy was reduced to a blackened, charred skeleton. "Everything that would burn did. I don't imagine the transport office found it very funny, nor did Rod, but boy did Lou, Bill and myself have a good laugh after the Norton burnt itself out. The look on Rod's face! Bill told Rod, along with explaining to Transport what had happened, he was to get four requisition slips for new jerkins!"

At times, the streets of England can seem mighty narrow to a young man from Manitoba, as Lou Lapointe discovered. "One morning, I was riding to CRE and came around a corner at about sixty miles per hour and there was a British truck passing another." Lapointe chose to take his chances with a fence over that of a head-on collision. "Well sir, I woke up in the hospital with a fractured skull. Stripped the bike down both sides. They had to write it off."

> September 19, 1941. It is becoming increasingly harder to get parts. Two m/cs have been held up in the shop for nearly three days for only minor replacements.
>
> September 30, 1941. Lt Morris spent most of the day trying to get m/c parts and tires from Field Stores, Aldershot.

Lapointe: "We were on a coal convoy and Hodgson couldn't get his bike started. I told him to catch up to us and I'd go and get the convoy lined up and on its way. There was a curve just as you got to the compound. Hodgson was coming hell bent for election, frozen on his bike. I recognized the situation so I tried to distract him by swerving one way and then the other. But he was bound he was going to hit me and he did. I rolled with the blow and came out okay but Hodgson was a little worse for wear."

Ross Hutton was posted to D Company HQ 17 July 1942, and Lapointe was assigned the task of teaching him how to ride. "He came from Minnedosa, Manitoba. Just a kid, sixteen years old, full of piss and vinegar. After a couple of days, I turned him out on his own. One day, I was riding along with him when we came to a T junction in the road at about forty miles per. He laid his bike down on its side, slid into the curb, then gunned it and landed back on his wheels again and kept right on going! I told him how lucky he was to get out of that one and he said, 'Oh hell, I do that all the time.'

"The next day, I came to another T junction. Well sir, I hit that curb and went flying into a big stone wall. I was all cuts and bruises and that was it for the little Norton. Then we were issued Harley 45s. They were a nice machine after we got used to them.

"Ross and I met coming back from a trip. We were discussing this and that about the 45s, so I said to him, 'Did you ever ride it standing up on the seat?' So I stood up on the seat and he did the same. Everything was going great until I turned around and spotted the provost after us. I got away, but they caught Ross. It cost him fourteen pounds."

Not all of Lapointe's misadventures ended so lightly. On 16 January 1942 Lapointe was assigned to escort four trucks of C Company to the demolition grounds and back. "They told me to return at 1600 hrs. I got back there at about 1530 hrs and the trucks were just lining up to go. I was about three hundred yards away from the lead truck when it exploded! The guy holding the detonators in the 15-cwt truck with the gelignite explosives aboard had dropped them. There wasn't enough left of the guy to bother picking up. It was a heck of a mess." The truck's driver died in hospital one day later.

Hodgson: "We were constructing a bomber station up at St. Eval in Cornwall, and I

**DR Ed Smith shows that the wide handlebars of a Harley-Davidson present no problem in negotiating a Canadian Army Motor Pool parking lot in England.**

would have a lot of runs to CRE, who at that time had their HQ in Leatherhead, Surrey. I was seeing a young lady then who resided in the small village of Great Bookham." Coincidently, these runs had to go right through Bookham, and although despatches were stamped with the time sent and received, a clever DR could always find a little free time via imaginary flat tires or chains mysteriously breaking, plausible delays that a rider could not be charged for (DRs were, however, charged for running out of gas).

During this despatch-run romance of Bookham, Hodgson was riding a Harley-Davidson, which had wider handlebars than the British bikes. "As I didn't dare park the bike out in front of the young lady's home for fear of the provost seeing it, I would bump the front gate open with my front tire, and then more or less swing the handlebars from side to side to clear the narrow gate, ride down the path and park around the back of the house.

"This one time, when I finally got the bike through the gate, I couldn't figure out why all of a sudden my machine was making such a strange noise. When I turned around to see what was causing the racket, I noticed that the bike kickstarter pedal had got caught in between two of the pickets on the gate, and I was now dragging the gate along beside me down the concrete path. I stopped and leaned it up against the hedge which ran alongside the path. The young lady's father came home from work that evening and mentioned to her that he believed she had a visitor that day!

"On another run, it was a lousy wet and cold day. When I got to the house soaking wet, the young lady's mother asked me if I would like some dried egg on toast and the ever-present tea. Of course, I didn't refuse."

In such congenial surroundings, Hodgson's mind was not on things military. "When I left, I wasn't too far up the road when I realized I had forgotten my web belt plus my revolver, a .38 Smith and Wesson. And I didn't have time to turn around and get it."

To make matters worse, he did not get the return run to CRE. "I was just hoping that we wouldn't have an armouries inspection while 'ye olde' gun was sitting in a private home down in Bookham. Rod made the next run to Leatherhead, so he picked it up for me. Anyway, I got away with another small escapade unscathed."

Hodgson's proficiency at the latter probably played a part in his being awarded a Good Conduct Badge 3 August 1942.

> January 8, 1943. The convoy was again split up in the darkness chiefly because of the shortage of DRs.
>
> February 1, 1943. Fog and ice. No vehicle including m/cs to be used except for essential services of high priority.
>
> June 25, 1943. Hodgson attached to HQ Coy Transport Section.

Hodgson: "I was assigned to an officer who was acting as an umpire for some Canadian units on a scheme. The officer's job was to tear ahead of convoys and check the times the convoys passed designated areas and the spacing of the vehicles. The officer had a driver and an 8-cwt truck. I would stay right on the truck's tail until the officer needed me to take a message to the provost. We were barrelling along a lovely narrow country road, just getting into a curve. A convoy of tanks was parked along the side of the road and coming at us was a convoy of trucks which wasn't supposed to be there."

Hodgson was unable to see in front of the truck he was following, and the driver did not have time to give "the usual slow-down sign. The 8-cwt had to brake really violently to avoid a head on with the lead convoy truck. I never even got a chance to hit my brakes. The Norton wedged under the truck and I went flying into the back. No real damage to myself but the poor old Norton didn't fare as well."

Despite the fact that the Norton's forks were cracked and the headlight and front fender smashed, Hodgson convinced the officer to give him a work ticket to ride it back to St. Eval: "It took me three days to get back, stopping at different unit camps for petrol, grub and a place for the night." Of course Hodgson also stopped to see his girl in Bookham.

The War Diary notes that in June of 1943 Lapointe was posted from Battalion Headquarters to Headquarters Company.

"When I was transferred to HQ as the colonel's personal DR, things started to happen. I hated that colonel so much I didn't even care to remember his name. Like one Saturday afternoon he sent me right across England just to deliver a message to a friend of his to meet him in London that night. It was raining cats and dogs, which it always was over there. I rode twelve hundred miles for that, right through London on them darn cobblestone roads. My ass was so sore when I got back! From that day on, the colonel and I just did not see eye-to-eye.

"So when time came to go to France, I got smart like a fox and got me a transfer to RCEME [Royal Canadian Electrical and Mechanical Engineers] driving one of those forty-ton Diamond T trucks, you know, ten wheels on the tractor and twenty-four wheels on the trailer. Then a DR went on leave. God forbid, they called on me to take his place!"

The need for proper training was obvious, yet not always given the priority it deserved. In an attempt to address the problem, the following notice appeared in several Battalion Orders during April of 1943:

> Lack of sufficient training and experience on the part of motorcyclists is a principal factor in the incidence of accidents. This is particularly so during exercises when frequent reliefs are necessary and road and weather conditions not always favourable. Commanding Officers will give their personal attention to the training of motorcyclists within their respective units. No officer or other rank will be detailed for motorcycle duties until he has completed an organized unit or other course of training and has been tested to the satisfaction of a qualified instructor.

**Typical Algonquin Regiment DRs on training.**

In both Canada and abroad, training continued throughout the war, with the emphasis on developing off-road riding skills. Arduous tests were devised to challenge Canada's future DRs. For example, in late 1944, a group of motorcyclists in training with the Algonquin Regiment stationed in North Bay, Ontario, rode an abandoned settlers' trail from Restoule to Spring Creek. These bikes are the only motorized wheeled vehicles on record to complete the twelve kilometres of blackflies, bog and bush.

## SGT-MAJ TOM JEFFERY

Algonquin Regiment, 4th Canadian Armoured Division

"Due to my position as transport sergeant, I felt it was my requirement to become as efficient as possible in all operations of the motorcycle, and with no intent to brag, I feel that I accomplished this. I like to think I am right when I say that the bikers of today, with all their huge machines and attachments, could not hold a candle to the bike riders of the last war."

Strong words. They come from a man born in a small northern Ontario community to a family of eleven children. But then, such an atmosphere usually breeds strong words.

On 29 July 1940, at age twenty-three, Jeffery enlisted with A Company of the Algonquin Regiment. He had already been out in the working world for eight years, first at a lumber camp when fifteen, and then at a saw mill in South River, Ontario, driving a lumber truck.

Army life in Canada took him to nearby Huntsville for a month, then to Camp Borden, and then to Port Arthur (Thunder Bay), where he was promoted to transportation sergeant. By June of 1941, he left Ontario for Camp Shilo in Manitoba where the Algonquin Transport Section completed their initial driver and mechanical training.

"It was at Camp Shilo that we first obtained a fleet of motorcycles, all of which were Indians, some equipped with sidecars. Of course, we had lots of fun with the sidecars. After some practice, I could lift the car several feet off the ground, with a passenger and going at a fair rate of speed!"

By mid-November, Jeffery was on the move again, this time to Niagara-on-the-Lake for the winter, "guarding Niagara Falls. I carry a distinct scar on my left cheek as a lasting memory of this area. While travelling on an icy back road to Allanburg, I applied the brakes on a curve, the front wheel locked, and the bike and I ended up alongside a barbed wire fence, my face torn."

Next stop was Truro, Nova Scotia, where Jeffery got his first ride on a Harley-Davidson. "We were running long convoys travelling at forty miles per hour on good highways. In order to get from the rear to the front of sixty or more vehicles, you required

**Above: Cpl Tom Jeffery aboard an Indian Chief at Camp Shilo, Manitoba.**

DR Osie Shanks models a leather kidney belt, 3 November 1941.

considerable speed. These Harleys had a low-compression cylinder head and the maximum speed was sixty-five miles per hour. The result was that I burned the motor on the machine I was operating. To correct this, I had the mechanics grind down the cylinder head on the new engine.

"Our next move (during the summer of 1942) was to Newfoundland where we uncrated thirty-two brand-new Harleys. The terrain was extremely rough and many a rider, myself included, ended up in a mud hole underneath these huge machines."

The War Diary entry for 13 August shows that "Capt L. C. Montri by leaning his m/c suddenly on the road from Grand Falls caused minor damage to his epidermis and battle dress trousers."

It was in Newfoundland that the kidney belt made its first appearance with the Regiment. "This was a wide leather belt worn around the waist and usually decorated with brass studs. No doubt it gave some support to the rider, but after consulting with some more qualified personnel, including our medical officer, I made all the bike riders stop wearing them. I was told that the continuous use would eventually weaken the back. You can believe I was not a very popular transport sergeant for a while."

Official opinion was to change and the kidney belt became mandatory wear in some outfits.

By January 1943 Jeffery was back in Truro, and then on the eleventh, he sailed for England aboard the *Empress of Scotland*, bound eventually for Heathfield, Sussex, where he was introduced to "the famous Norton, and driving on the wrong side of the road." A "m/c refresher course under Sergeant McNeil" held in late July helped to acquaint DRs with these new bikes and the peculiarities of English roads.

On 24 October the Algonquins were issued the first rum ration in Canadian military history. Nine months later, the Regiment was in France, fighting the enemy instead of hangovers. Outside Caen, near Hubert Folie, roads and fields had been churned up by an armoured blender of tanks, heavy trucks, mines, and artillery fire. Eight inches of dehydrated soil lay loose on the earth, choking the hot August air. Canadian guns continually pounded at the enemy, firing low into the haze. Jeffery and his Norton raced through the smoke and the noise, passing under the barrels of the big guns. "There was a huge explosion and the next thing I was blown off the bike!"

Tanks charged into battle, the crews peering through a thick veil of dust, searching for a distant enemy. Jeffery knew he lay unseen, lost in the storm of the battle. "I thought, this is it, I will be run over by our own tanks!" He looked up and saw the muzzle of an 18-pounder artillery gun rocking back and forth from the recoil. He had passed just under the muzzle as the gun had fired, the force knocking him down. He quickly picked up his Norton and rode to safer ground.

"The Norton was the most efficient bike of them all, not too big but like a stubborn mule you could load everything that you could tie on it and it never left you stranded."

After the battles of Falaise area, the 4th Armoured Division advanced up the coast of France pursuing an enemy in rapid retreat. Demands upon the DRs increased greatly.

> The convoy broke into fragments repeatedly, and it was only by the superhuman efforts of the DRs and RPs [Regimental Police] that any coherence at all was maintained. Some of the DRs had to be relieved on their jobs because they were literally blinded by dust.[24]

"We had been driving for three days and nights without rest and taking pills to stay awake." Occasionally, the huge convoy would stop, but the troops never knew for how long; sometimes it would be for minutes, sometimes for hours. At one point, "we had been stopped for some time, waiting in the darkness and the pouring rain. I put my bike on its stand, crawled into the back of a 15-cwt truck, and fell asleep."

Jeffery awoke to find the convoy moving. How long he had been asleep, or how far this motorized mobile bed had taken him, he did not know, yet he still leapt out into the darkness to find his prized Norton. This was one of those rare occasions Jeffery was pleased to discover how little sleep he had managed to steal between rides, as fortunately the convoy had not travelled far.

When the 4th Armoured Division crossed into Germany at Cleve during February of 1945, Jeffery found a surprise waiting for him—an abandoned BMW, its keys still in the ignition: "It was surely the Cadillac of motorcycles. I had never even heard of a shaft-drive bike. I kept it for about two weeks and just loved riding it."

Near the end of the second week, Jeffery and his newly acquired mount were on a run up to the front lines where the infantry was dug in. It was dark, and the troops could not see Jeffery's approach. They only heard the distinctive sound of the BMW motor coming towards them. To their trained ears, that sound meant enemy!

The soldiers called out for Jeffery to halt, but he did not hear. The troops opened fire, the flash of their rifles spitting out into the night. "It did not take me long to hit the dirt. I was advised to get rid of the bike. It was with tears in my eyes that I finally disposed of it for several bottles of Loud Mouth."

It was not unusual for the retreating enemy to abandon equipment. What was unusual about Jeffery's find was that the BMW had not been rigged to explode when started.

Promoted to sergeant major, Jeffery stayed on as part of the Canadian Army Occupation Force after the war, but, in accordance with Canadian military tradition, had to give up the bike that never left him stranded to become a commissioned officer, ending his career as a DR.

LAC Collier, RCAF, aboard a rare sidecar-equipped Norton 16H.

The number of motorcycles in each regiment varied depending upon the regiment's role. The average infantry regiment could have as many as fifteen motorcycles assigned to HQ Company. Armoured and artillery regiments might have fewer. The serious users of motorcycles were the RCCS and the Provost Corps, a typical transport section for each consisting of a three-ton truck and about twenty-five motorcycles. The Intelligence Corps also made extensive use of motorcycles, relying on the machines' superior mobility to get them into battle-torn areas quickly as the infantry advanced.

Even the RCAF ground crews used bikes as a speedy means to collect intelligence information and photographs from incoming aircraft and then deliver the documents to HQ. The RCAF DR also did parts runs. The bikes were identified by squadron number and logo or air force roundel. RCAF officers often purchased or borrowed civilian bikes to ride to aircraft flight sections, briefings and scheduled air tests.

The uniform of a DR attached to the RCCS consisted of high leather boots, jodhpurs and a black or brown leather vest. Such DRs wore a winged-wheel patch on the left arm below the elbow, bearing the initials DR. This patch often caused confusion among soldiers of other Allied forces who frequently mistook it for a sergeant major's insignia of rank, much to the amusement of the Canadian riders.

Two officers of the 407 Sqn, RCAF, aboard their own machines, F-O Eric Cameron on a 1937 350 cc Velocette and F-O Charles Thompson on a 500 cc OHV BSA single, riding through the snow of Scotland while looking quite dapper in regulation fleece-lined, leather flying jackets and leather flying boots.

No. 1 Provost Company was formed from volunteers taken from the ranks of the RCMP. Initially, this unit wore the RCMP insignia as a shoulder flash and cap badge in combination with the regulation battle dress. By mid-1940, non-RCMP riders were being accepted into the outfit, so the RCMP insignia was

**Pte Larry Liscumb proudly displays a typical DR outfit. The Harley-Davidson is an early-pattern WLC.**

dropped. The standard provost uniform was distinguished by its white webbed waist and shoulder belt, white pistol holster with a neck cord attached to the pistol butt, and white gauntlet gloves. The letters *MP* were usually painted on the front of the helmet and were also displayed upon an arm band worn on the upper left sleeve.

Riders in other outfits wore uniforms varying as much by the company they were attached to as by whatever miscellaneous items they were able to scrounge.

An important and welcome addition was made to the uniform late in 1944: "Effective immediately, winter underwear, long, as issued, will be taken into wear."

The DR's uniform was a popular and sought-after one, even by non-riders, which led to this notice of 17 July 1941: "All leather jerkins and canvas trousers and jackets not being used by DRs employed as such are to be turned into Btn QM stores not later than 15/Aug."

The Westminster Regiment Battalion Orders for 12 June 1942 included the latest fashion note:

> The present motorcyclist's protective clothing consisting of jackets and leggings, proofed, will be superseded by coats, rubber, proofed, motor, cyclist (catalogue No. CH0521-0532) when existing stocks are exhausted. These coats which have been thoroughly tested under varying weather conditions are so made that the tail may be brought up through the crotch and buttoned over the stomach and around each leg. Strong press studs are provided for this purpose.

No. 1 Provost Company on maintenance training in England, 1940. The RCMP arm bands and badges were soon to replaced by Provost insignia.

Typical Provost uniform, England, 1 February 1944.

**No. 1 Provost Company in rubber riding gear on Convoy Patrol Roll Call, England, 1942.**

By 1945, some pointsmen were issued with duffle coats. Badges of rank were to be worn on "overalls; blouses, denim; and jackets, motorcyclist."

Owing to the limited carrying-capacity of a motorcycle, the rider was not as well equipped to defend himself from enemy attack as other Canadian soldiers. In England, riders carried a Smith and Wesson .38 or Enfield Mk 1 .38 revolver, but this was upgraded to either a Sten gun or Thompson machine gun prior to the invasion of Europe, except for the Provost Corps which continued to carry revolvers. Unfortunately, the Sten gun had a reputation for discharging occasionally when the motorcycle hit a bump, and a rider under fire usually couldn't afford the time to stop and set up the Thompson, so it was not uncommon to see non-Provost riders switching back to revolvers. Some continued to favour the Thompson, though, as it was reportedly good for opening wine barrels.

The revolvers were not totally ineffectual as a means of defence, as Lance Corporal Blackmore and Lance Corporal Moss of the 4th Provost Company discovered. Ambushed by thirty enemy troops carrying rifles and machine guns, the two provost had their motorcycles shot out from under them. Refusing to surrender, they not only defended themselves until help arrived, they also carried an injured comrade through a wheat field, all the while returning fire with their revolvers. Blackmore and Moss both received a Military Medal for their efforts.

Two pieces of equipment common to all riders and loathed by most were the crash helmet and goggles. The original pulp helmet, so named because it was made from a hardened papier-mâché, was bowl-shaped and sat high on the rider's head, positioned there by an inner sling. The sling was supposed to rest on the top of the skull, providing a space between the head and helmet for shock absorption. In 1943, this lightweight, but not overly effective, helmet was replaced by the Steel Helmet, DR Mk I, a much heavier and subsequently greatly despised alternative. The Part I Orders for #2 MAC, RCASC, were typical of the change:

> Authority is granted for the issue of 5306 Helmets, Steel, DR, Mk I on the scale of one for each motorcycle in unit establishment. A very high proportion of injuries resulting from motorcycle accidents are fractured skulls and other head injuries. The wearing of Helmets, Steel, DR, Mk I will therefore be compulsory for all officers and DRs travelling by motorcycle or sidecar either as driver or as passenger. Before passing a helmet of any type from one individual to another, it will be disinfected by sponging all parts which come into contact with the hair or skin of the wearer with a solution of Izal and water and drying by exposure to air.

**A Provost in regulation uniform, his pulp helmet largely ineffective for anything more than minor impacts.**

It was not uncommon for a rider to remove the uncomfortable steel helmet and store it on the bike once out of range of unit HQ. Warnings such as, "Mobile Patrols are paying special attention to members of 1st Canadian Army operating m/cs without crash helmets and the carriage of unauthorized passengers," began to show up frequently on Part I Orders. One went so far as to suggest that not wearing a helmet "may prejudice any claim for pension in the event of death or injury." The regularity of such warnings while the Canadian troops were stationed in England verged on monotony.

Regulation goggles were small and round, allowing almost no peripheral vision. With these came an "anti-fogging paste," with the emphasis on paste rather than anti-fog. When the goggles were clean, the sun reflecting off the lenses made an excellent target for enemy snipers, while dusty roads rendered the lenses nearly opaque from the filth. Most riders preferred to risk painful eye irritations and punitive action rather than to ride blind or be shot at. As a result, the motorcyclist, army, again made the pages of battalion Part I Orders: "Discipline, M/C drivers: Effective immediately, all m/c drivers of this unit will wear goggles."

Frowned upon by CMHQ at the beginning, the wearing of kidney belts, also referred to as body belts, was eventually made mandatory by some outfits when injuries sustained from the absence of such devices began to appear after a few years of pounding aboard wartime motorcycles with limited suspension movement. Other units tolerated the belts as long as they were kept under the uniform, not on top, and "belts cannot be embellished with Reg't badges, etc."

## PTE ART GAIGER

2nd Canadian Motor Ambulance Corps, RCASC

"It seemed we almost never got off the bicycles those days. It was ride the three miles to and from Danforth Technical School, have supper, and get on the Tamblyn's Drug Store bikes from six to eleven for fifty cents each night. Small wonder I dreamed of becoming a motorcyclist."

War had been declared, and Gaiger's father and brother had already enlisted. "I was getting the feeling of being left behind, anxious to get into the army and do my bit." But Gaiger was not of age yet, and had to wait until March of 1943 before joining up.

Advanced training at Camp Borden, Ontario, brought him a little closer to his motorcycling dream when he enrolled in a four-week motorcycle course. When he turned nineteen, he was posted overseas, then attached to 2nd Canadian Motor Ambulance Corps (CMAC) RCASC in Hythe, England, on 2 May 1944. "This was an ambulance unit. It was designed to function between FDS [Field Dressing Stations] and CCS [Casualty Clearing Stations]."

In this unit, as in most at the time, all the DR jobs were filled by seasoned people. "I was assigned as a spare driver on an ambulance in A Company, resigned to stay there forever."

However, shortly after his section landed in Normandy on 10 July 1944, an unexpected opportunity presented itself. "We were in convoy, passing through the pocket of the Falaise Gap, following the armoured units of 3rd Division. There were long waits through the day while bulldozers cleared the roads of the dead, both horses and men."

**Above: Moose Ferrier and a smiling Art Gaiger near Calais, France, 1944.**

During one such holdup, Gaiger's ambulance eased up beside an abandoned Norton lying on its side in a ditch, its rear tire flat. At the time, an ambulance seemed like a logical place for an ailing motorcycle, so Gaiger and the ambulance driver loaded the bike into the back. "Our platoon officer, Lieutenant Bayly, fancied himself a motorcyclist, so he commissioned me to paint out the markings on the bike, and from then on, to ride it as a 3rd Platoon DR when we were moving."

Coincidentally perhaps, the 2nd CMAC War Diary entry for 11 October 1944 warned that the practice of units stealing vehicles from other units was "scorned upon."

"Riding on daily convoys was exciting, and sort of made me feel important, a feeling privates don't often get. The job was to ride ahead, ensure that the roads were not destroyed or blocked, and report back frequently to the leading jeep with the officer in it. At intersections, it was traffic control, turning the trucks in the correct direction—ensuring they were still all there, and then passing to the front again to check with the officer."

As 2nd CMAC, 3rd Platoon, did not travel in the front lines, contact with the enemy was not considered likely or anticipated. Security in the outfit was relaxed. This serenity was broken in September 1944.

"We had been in camp outside Ypres, Belgium, for about an hour. The latrine was dug, the fires lit, and dinner under way, when two Belgian civilians rode up excitedly proclaiming that an enemy infantry column had been bypassed by the Polish Armour, and was moving toward us!

"Panic set in about what to do, and very quickly the officer ordered a withdrawal back into France. We were not a combat unit, but all except the medical corps men were issued with Sten guns, and we had one .303 rifle that someone had picked up along the way. The Sten guns had not been oiled and the magazines of ammunition were dusty, with some rust showing. The best clips of ammo were selected and assigned to the DRs, who were responsible to ride ahead along separate roads, and if contact was made with the enemy, to attempt to return and warn the platoon."

Gaiger rode his Norton uneasily along his assigned route, but finding no sign of the enemy, returned. By then, 3rd Platoon had packed up and gone, with not so much as a hint as to where or which way. This left Gaiger in a serious predicament. Had his outfit fled east, with the enemy in hot pursuit? Or perhaps they had chosen their route based on information brought back by one of the other DRs, and maybe, as he sat there, the enemy was advancing upon him, charging up the very road shunned by his own platoon. Gaiger decided to head back toward Ypres.

Potentially, the enemy could be anywhere. Gaiger rode past Poperinge with no enemy encounters. Then, as he approached Ypres, the infamous infantry column appeared, marching orderly, rifles slung, with one Polish soldier following behind, machine gun at the ready. "These, the enemy soldiers earlier reported as heading our way, were just looking for someone to surrender to."

Eventually reunited with his outfit, Gaiger's next harrowing adventure took place outside a brothel in the village of Hardinghen. Actually, technically speaking, it began inside, and following "some wonderful moments that took me from virginity and transformed me into a normal nineteen-year-old private who never abandoned thereafter the quest for wine, women, and song," he struck up a conversation with a private who had also just paid his respects to this establishment. The two of them waited upon less hurried friends, and "after some time, the private said he would keep an eye on my Norton if I wanted to hustle up my friend, and I accepted his offer." Gaiger never saw the Norton again.

This put quite a cramp in his DR career, not to mention his new-found hobby, but after several months of double duty, an opportunity came up to get back in the saddle again. A promotion had left a DR position open at HQ in Nijmegen and, contrary to the earlier days, there were no volunteers. Cold weather had now engulfed Europe. His debt to the army now paid, Gaiger got the job.

"I had been back for only a few days when we traded in the Nortons for brand-new Harley-Davidsons. We took the Harleys out in small groups when possible to get used to them, as not many of us had Harley experience. There were precise breaking-in instructions for new motors in those days, and the plan was to log some time at low speeds on the very good roads around Nijmegen.

"On my first day out, I went with Sgt "Cue-Ball" Leonard and Cpl Les Hopley, anticipating close adherence to the rules, although having known these guys for awhile, I shouldn't have been surprised when they started to race each other. We reached speeds of eighty miles per hour that day, doubtlessly dooming the machines then and there.

"The DR job in Nijmegen consisted of a routine daily two-mile run to HQ for mail and documents, with an occasional special run. However, our outfit had an obligation along with other platoons in 2nd CMAC to provide a DR for the Deputy Director of Medical Services (DDMS). I was sent down the road ten miles to be that DR for one month.

**An unidentified DR on a Harley-Davidson in Eindhoven, Holland, December 1944. Note that the toolbox is missing from the front fender and that the horn is now located above the headlight, indicative of a later-pattern WLC (post mid-1941).**

"This job kept me on the road most of the day. It entailed delivering and receiving packages to and from various officials, including Gen Guy Simonds. One cold day, I thought I would freeze to death on my run, so in desperation, I rode up a long lane to a Dutch farmhouse and asked if I could come in." After some time spent sipping coffee around a pot-belly stove, Gaiger was off again.

"Another day, it was very icy and I was completing my run along the sidewalk of the town near DDMS HQ when a 60-cwt lorry began a left turn across my path, about one hundred feet ahead. I couldn't stop, but with that huge truck about to arrive exactly where I was headed, I started to feather the brakes. It didn't work and I skidded on to my left side, the bike and I continuing toward the truck, sliding along the ice at about fifteen miles per hour.

"The driver, God bless him, must have caught a glimpse of my approach. He skidded to a stop right in front of me so that his front tire took the force of the impact. Had he not seen me, I would have slid under the truck between the wheels and likely got all ground up."

Some of Gaiger's missions, like fetching a dozen burgers for the DDMS staff, or picking up an officer's spare tunic left at a tailoring shop a couple of weeks prior, were pretty mundane. Others, like chasing down an ambulance that had mistakenly turned toward the front with a full load of wounded, weren't as easy. "I caught up with him about a quarter of a mile short of the enemy, and turned him around."

The platoon had another DR, "Jeff 'Showboat' Daigle, who always took off with a roar. One time, we heard him race up through the gears as he left camp, followed by a tremendous crash just around the bend. A truck had suddenly pulled out of a field, and Jeff hit it dead on. He broke both his legs, and some other bones too. His war was over.

"I then took his run out to HQ. On the return trip, the unit had moved forward again, so it was hide-and-seek time once more."

After a run-in with a half-track during convoy duty that sent him and the Harley sprawling across the pavement, leaving him bleeding and semi-conscious with a dented crash helmet and bent bike, all followed by a bawling out for smashing the bike, Gaiger was now firmly convinced he had a "thankless and totally idiotic job. The action of the steel helmet on my head had been causing hair loss by the handful, my kidneys were shook up by the constant jarring, and despite my begging for a windscreen to ease the discomforts, I was denied this luxury with flimsy excuses like 'If you ever go over the handlebars, your head will get cut off!' I was fed up with being a DR!"

On 10 April 1945 Gaiger resigned as an army motorcyclist and finished his days in service as he had begun, driving an ambulance.

Ted Picknell pilots a Norton Big 4 while stationed in England.

As for the motorcycles, although the Allied war offices drew up specifications for dedicated military machines, the resulting bikes were heavy and cumbersome. The 500 cc BSA Model J12 (developed prior to the outbreak of the Second World War) was typical of the breed, and fortunately only a few Canadians, principally those serving with the RCAF ground crews in North Africa, were subjected to its quirks.

Norton's answer to WD specifications was the Big 4, a 633 cc armoured sidecar unit. Its main role in Canadian forces was as a substitute for unavailable armoured vehicles during patrols and exercises in England.

The US manufacturers made a few experimental war bikes too, the Harley-Davidson XA, patterned after the BMW, and the 750 cc Indian transverse V-twin being the main contenders. Both were tested by Capt Bernie Nicholson and Lt-Col Tony Miller at the Barriefield Training Centre and found to be unsuitable for military use because of excessive weight and complexity. The most successful motorcycles were the tried-and-true bikes of pre-war civilian use. More reliable, faster and better handling than any military motorcycle to date, there was no mistaking these machines for "bicycles fitted with motors." Suspensions, or more precisely, the lack thereof, were the new motorcycles' only real sore point, and also the riders' for that matter. Bumps out back were still handled solely by saddle springs, while the front suspension on most makes consisted of a crude set of levers and rods that offered precious little movement, the majority of abuse from war-ravaged roads being absorbed by the tires, frame and rider.

Capt Bernie Nicholson road tests a Harley-Davidson XA leading a group of DR trainees on WLCs near Kingston, Ontario, 1940.

## PTE JACK AISBITT

3rd Anti-Tank Regiment, RCA

"I suppose in our unit there were eight or ten men who were DRs at times but quit for one reason or another, some in accidents, others when the novelty wore off. I was the only one who stayed on as a rider through to the end of the war.

"In England, the independence as a DR was great, being able to take off and visit where you wanted with no one the wiser. In Europe, it was dangerous, less places to go, less time, but still I was independent and able to slip away at times. But it was a lonely job after 6 June 1944."

Aisbitt enlisted 18 October 1940, "one month before my eighteenth birthday," and seventeen days after the formation of his regiment. At Debert, Nova Scotia, he trained as a DR, then was shipped overseas in October 1941 aboard the *Andes*. Although his training had been on an Indian, when he got to England, he rode a Norton, and also a Harley for a brief spell, which he found "much more comfortable than the Norton but too heavy to handle in cross-country riding." The Norton he considered "an extremely durable machine that seemed to go forever with no problems of any consequence."

Some might consider him lucky with British bikes, but not so with British walls. While stationed at Denne Park, near Billingshurst, Aisbitt "ran into a stone wall in Sussex and broke my helmet (no plastic in those days). Fortunately, it was only a mild concussion."

British cows were a problem too. After delivering a night-time message to one of the batteries located in an old farmhouse, Aisbitt began retracing his run, "too fast, of course," down the long lane that led in from the main road. The path was dark and lined with mature trees. "A large shape loomed up in front of me. At the last split second before

**Above: Punctures were a frequent and deflating experience for busy DRs like Jack Aisbitt.**

impact, I recognized it—a cow's ass!" Aisbitt struck this imposing target smack-dab centre, flying over the handlebars and, fortunately, the animal's hindquarters too. It was a startled beast that disappeared back into the night.

"I managed to get the bike back up to the house where I had my scrapes and bruises tended to and handlebars straightened. The front of the bike was splashed with cow dung! You can bet the boys had a great laugh over that one when I returned to my own unit."

There were more casualties among DRs resulting from accidents than direct contact with the enemy. It was the nature of the job, dodging in and out of trucks and tanks while herding night-time convoys over muddy, rough roads with only the glint of a blacked-out headlight to illuminate the way.

"Army vehicles in convoy have an accordion effect as they try to keep evenly spaced. Parts of the convoy are going like hell, while those in front may be slowing rapidly due to some hold-up. This results in a particular hazard for a rider as he tries to duck back in between vehicles while passing to avoid oncoming traffic. A rider had to become proficient at laying the bike down and sliding under the truck, otherwise you were face first into the tailgate. A very good pal, Morley Hicks, an orphan, was killed in a head on while passing in 1943 while we were in England.

"I landed at Courseulles-Sur-Mer, France, D+2, off a LCT [Landing Craft, Tank] with the bike and myself in the back of a truck, joining the first echelon which had landed on D-Day.

"The advance was quite rapid at times and we would move to new positions every two or three days. Because of the possibility of running over mines, it was the practice when crossing fields in a line of vehicles for the DR to follow in the tire tracks of a truck ahead. On one occasion, the truck ahead of me ran over a mine, blowing its right front apart. Fortunately, it was a small mine and there were no injuries other than shock to the occupants of the truck. As I had been travelling in the right track as well, I too was pretty well shook up because if the truck had not tripped that mine, I would have, with probably more serious results."

The first month in France saw Aisbitt's regiment right in the thick of battle, inexperienced and not yet wise to the ways of war, fighting a seasoned enemy in the Caen-Carpiquet airport area. "I was taking a message to one of our battery HQs near a village called Cairon or Thaon, I think. My map was useless—nothing looked as it should."

A lone provost stood at an intersection that had become known as Hell's Corners, directing a rush of tanks and truck traffic while intermittent shellfire exploded around him. Aisbitt rode up through the mayhem and asked which way to "Thaon." In the noise and confusion, the decidedly rattled provost pointed left toward Caen and the enemy.

Behind the immediate front line of battle there is often as much as a mile of unearthly quiet, where the signs of very recent fighting fester in eerie silence, smothering the world in a battle's aftermath. Aisbitt was not "fully tuned in to this yet."

He rode swiftly, bouncing along a road without traffic, past the still-burning remains of bombed-out Bren carriers, past the shattered and smoking stubs of telephone poles, and past the bodies of fallen men. A soldier knelt in silence beside a new grave.

The DR rode on, uneasy and unsure, still carrying his message to battery HQ. The farther he advanced, the more vivid became the signs of human conflict, the blood of its victims still red on grimy uniforms. "I believe it was the Queen's Own Rifles in action. Had it not been for the motor noise of the Norton, I probably would have heard rifle and machine-gun fire."

**DRs often relied upon Provosts for directions during the confusion of battle. Sgt T. S. Giles of No. 4 Provost Company points the way for Cpl Philippe Castoilloux, Régiment de la Chaudière, Normandy, France, 15 June 1944.**

Instead, he heard nothing. He followed the road, steering his Norton around the debris, and then around a bend, and . . . stomp on and grab that Norton's brakes! A downed motorcycle blocked his path. Beside it, a fellow DR, sprawled out and lifeless. He caught sight of two infantry men behind a roadside sign waving frantically with their arms, motioning him back and away.

"I skidded the bike around and went like hell back the way I came. To this day, I can imagine the bullets whistling by me, although I do not know if I was being shot at or not. I never got caught in that situation again."

But he did experience closer contact with the enemy. Mid-September, "a pal and fellow rider, Joe Lerrette, and I were making some tea in a farmyard near Bolougne at about 6 a.m. We were the only ones around. Then down the road and through the gate came an enemy soldier, about thirty-five to forty, fat and shaking, hands over his head. Behind him, a very small French farmer followed, covering the soldier with his own Schmeisser machine gun. The Frenchman had a smile on his face a yard wide. The soldier was having an anxiety attack.

"Joe spoke some French and found out that the soldier had been hiding out in the rain for a few days, was starving, and had been afraid to give himself up to the Canadians. He had approached the Frenchman who assured him he would be okay, and then delivered the soldier to us. We thanked the Frenchman and tried to relieve him of the gun but he would not give it up, so we let him take it with him."

Aisbitt and his pal fed their prisoner and took his money, "French francs, no good to him now." The prisoner "wound up smiling and happy. He was out of it now. The last we saw of him, he was riding away in the back of the provost's jeep, looking back and waving goodbye, a smile on his face while eating bread. A hilarious sight if you ever saw one.

"In Belgium, myself and a fellow DR were taking our convoy to a new position a few miles away. We were leap-frogging, each taking our turn going to the front of the convoy to direct the vehicles down certain roads.

"As I was coming up from the back, I saw a sign pointing down a road reading Poperinge. I recalled that my father, who was a sergeant in the 75th Infantry Battalion in the first war, had often mentioned that town when I was a boy, so I was curious. I made the turn and rode down to the village, meaning to come right back. However, I got to talking to some English-speaking people, wound up in a tavern, had a few, and didn't get away until late afternoon."

Although Aisbitt thought he knew the way back, as evening swept away daylight, he became lost. "I wound up at some point in a large dark forest. I realized that there was no traffic, no signs of any troops or positions. I was totally alone.

"I became very alarmed, afraid of running into enemy positions, so pulled into the woods, sat under a tree, and listened. Absolute silence. I did this two or three times. Then, just as dawn broke, I came across what turned out to be a 2nd Division frontline position (I was 3rd Division). As I was approaching them from in front of the guards, I was challenged, with a rifle pointed at me and told in no uncertain terms not to move. A guard then summoned an officer, who, after questioning, sent me on my way toward 3rd Division. Eventually, I found my own 3rd Anti-Tank Regiment where I was soundly berated by the sergeant major, who did not believe one word of my being lost. I did not tell him of my detour into Poperinge, of course."

Aside from this unplanned adventure, Aisbitt remained with his regiment throughout the war, which ended for him in Emden, Germany. He was discharged in February 1946.

**F-O Johnny Williams bombs around in Burma on a Welbike, August 1944.**

Canada's unique position of being both a part of the British Commonwealth and a neighbour and close ally of the US allowed it the enviable opportunity to make use of motorcycles from both bike-producing countries. The Norton 16H, BSA M20 and Harley-Davidson WLC were the mainstays of Canadian riders. The Ariel, Indian (especially in sidecar guise), Matchless G3L, Royal Enfield and Triumph 3HW also saw some service in the Canadian forces. Midway through the war, ten Simplex Servicycles were employed in despatch duties within London. The Welbike, a collapsible machine designed to be dropped by parachute, saw limited official use by the 1st Canadian Parachute Battalion and even more limited unofficial use by a few RCAF personnel on joy rides.

The English bikes were considerably lighter and had more ground clearance than their US counterparts and were therefore the preferred mount for cross-country riding. The US makes were at their best on smoother roads in convoy and DR duty.

Early and later models of both the Norton 16H and the Harley-Davidson WLC were produced during the war. With one notable exception, the variations were minor. The exception concerned the hand controls on the WLC.

The hand controls on early-pattern Harley-Davidsons were designed to operate opposite to any other Allied bike. The throttle twistgrip was located on the left side of the handlebar (rather than the near universal right side) with the magneto advance/retard control on the right. The rationale for this break with tradition was that with this arrangement, a soldier could ride and shoot at the same time. How that soldier was supposed to cope with the recoil of a .38 revolver or Sten gun while bouncing at speed over bombed-out and debris-cluttered terrain was never explained. It was an unpopular system among both novices and experienced riders alike.

Ray Lehman, ex-president of the Black Hawks Motorcycle Club of Hamilton, Ontario, and lance corporal and DR attached to the 2nd CMAC, was one of the disenchanted riders who couldn't wait for the manufacturer or the military establishment to correct a flawed design: "I decided to convert my bike to right-hand throttle."

In so doing, Lehman reversed the direction of control, the throttle now opening with a clockwise rotation of the wrist. This "took just a bit of getting used to. One day, our transport officer asked me if he could borrow my bike to go into town. I explained the throttle change to him and suggested he take one of the other bikes."

Taking no heed of this sage advice, the officer started the bike and accelerated away. "He gave it too much throttle, and forgetting immediately what I had told him, twisted his hand to the right, giving it even more gas instead of cutting back. The bike took off from under him and he landed underneath one of the lorries. About a dozen of us

**Canadian riders posted at Trois-Rivières, Quebec, prepare for patrol duty along the St. Lawrence Seaway, March 1942.**

witnessed the whole thing and had quite a laugh out of it. He never did live down the entertainment he provided and he never asked to borrow my bike again. Shortly after this, our Workshop section modified all the throttles on our bikes to standard right-hand control with proper direction of rotation." Later pattern Harley-Davidsons were equipped with right-hand throttle controls before leaving the factory.

For the most part, military activity in Canada consisted of enlisting, initial training and shipping the troops to various fronts. Coastal patrols from land were also done, and key navigational routes, like the Welland Canal and St Lawrence Seaway, were continuously guarded. The economy of using motorcycles in this home defence, saving the more expensive armoured vehicles for overseas action, were obvious, even to the machines' detractors.

As volunteers poured into enlisting depots throughout Canada, British troops poured onto the Continent in an attempt to halt the enemy's advance. By 25 May 1940 this initial Allied action had been pushed back to the sea. Between 27 May and 4 June over 338,000 soldiers were evacuated from the beaches of Dunkirk, abandoning vast quantities of sorely needed equipment.

On 13 and 14 June a small party of Canadians from the 1st Infantry Brigade, 1st Field Regiment (RCHA), No. 1 Provost Company and other attached units from the 1st Canadian Division, landed at Brest. It was hoped that this small contingent of soldiers would be able to establish a beachhead on the coast of Brittany.

Three brothers, Douglas, Emerson and Sheldon Rogers, participated in the raid. They were all DRs, although Sheldon went without his bike, serving as a spare driver owing to an accident on his way to the docks in England. His disabled Norton stayed behind.

**Portrait of a DR Family. The Rogers brothers, Douglas, Emerson and Sheldon in England.**

French trains carried much of the Canadian infantry inland (toward Le Mans) to within twenty miles of the enemy's experienced troops as DRs guided the artillery and other equipment through crowded roads, cheered on by the enthusiastic and hopeful French.

Fortunately, the futility of the situation was recognized before any serious contact with the enemy was made. The troops were ordered to evacuate the area as quickly as possible. By then, roads were clogged with refugees dragging along whatever personal belongings they could cart with them. Canadian convoys at times sat idle, the route blocked so badly that even the motorcycles could not get through. Miraculously, the Canadians made it to the English Channel and from there to Aldershot, England, all within forty-eight hours of having set foot in France. Behind, they left 216 new vehicles, all destroyed before the enemy could take possession of them. Over a dozen motorcycles were run off the end of the dock, and gasoline was traded to citizens for wine.

Also left behind were six Canadians: Sgt D. G. Hutt of the RCCS, killed in a motorcycle accident; and five others taken as prisoners. One of the prisoners was Bob Creighton of Bancroft, Ontario. He had crashed his motorcycle while on convoy duty and was sent to a French hospital. On 22 June France surrendered. Creighton spent the next five years as a POW. The other four escaped captivity in 1941 and returned to England.

The shortage of armaments and transport, considered severe at the onset of war, was now desperate. Manufacturers simply could not fill the orders. Because the 1st Canadian Division was the best equipped of any of the Allied troops, it took over the primary role of defence of the British Isles. From the standpoint of a young nation's self-esteem, this was an important assignment. And so too, perhaps, seemed the defence of Hong Kong, one of the classic blunders of the Second World War. None other than Winston Churchill had conceded loss before the battle even began. On 7 January 1941, he wrote to General Ismay, "If Japan goes to war with us there is not the slightest chance of holding Hong Kong or relieving it. It is most unwise to increase the loss we shall suffer there."[25] Relying on British Intelligence for information, the Canadian army was not made aware of Churchill's views, although the threat was obvious. On 27 October 1941 the Winnipeg Grenadiers and the Royal Rifles, 1,975 Canadian soldiers in total, left Vancouver aboard the 570-passenger steamship *Awateo*, bound for Hong Kong as reinforcements to the ten thousand existing British troops.

Not on board were forty-five motorcycles left behind because of lack of space. An American ship, the *Don Jose*, steamed out of the Vancouver harbour 4 November, destination Hong Kong, the missing motorcycles and 167 other vehicles in its cargo hold. The freighter should have reached the British colony 6 December, but under orders of US naval authorities, it was rerouted to Manila. The vehicles ended up being used in the US defence of the Philippines.

Not that the shipment would have done the Canadians any more good than it did their American counterparts. On 7 December 1941 a sixty-thousand-strong enemy force attacked Hong Kong. On 25 December they had captured the island. Two hundred and ninety Canadians were dead. The rest, including 493 wounded, faced three and one half years of torture and starvation in foul prison camps that claimed the lives of yet another 267 Canadians.

There is not much that can be said about the short-lived battle or aftermath here, except that as the enemy pushed hard, the troops fought back with obsolete equipment in need of repair, and when ammunition ran out, they threw stones. Through all this, Lionel Speller, a DR with the RCCS, continued to ride his BSA delivering messages, riding over rough terrain, sometimes with one hand so that he could return fire from snipers with the other. For his efforts, he became one of the few Canadian DRs serving in the Second World War to be awarded the Military Medal:

> Cpl Speller deserves the highest praise for his performance during the engagement at Hong Kong. On December 19, 1941, he carried out his duties as Despatch Rider on the island between various Headquarters, often through fire swept areas. His main concern was the delivery of messages, and he showed utter lack of regard for his personal safety. He volunteered during his time off duty to accompany other riders to ensure messages getting through. During the course of his trips, he often travelled over strange ground which was occupied by guerillas friendly to the enemy. Despite the fact that one Despatch Rider was killed on the same road Cpl Speller travelled on several occasions, he continued to traverse this road on which he came under direct observation and fire of the enemy for a distance of more than a mile. Throughout the operation, he carried out all his duties and volunteered for additional difficult and dangerous tasks. He showed courage and devotion to duty above the ordinary and was an inspiration to all who came in contact with him.[26]

Since 1919, Canada had been asserting its independence as prudently as pride permitted. Indeed, it was this desire to be seen as an independent nation that precipitated the seven-day difference between Britain's declaration of war and Canada's. And it was this growing national pride that engendered a certain cockiness among its soldiers; a keenness to set themselves apart from the rest of the khaki crowd.

Perhaps the most visible reflection of this attitude was seen among Canada's DRs. It

**RCA DRs assist Dutch ladies through the streets of Amsterdam.**

was not long before they established a singularly Canadian DR identity. And reputation. On 17 April 1945 the late Peter Veldheer, a Dutch historian, witnessed the liberation of his village of Hoenderloo. He was fourteen at the time.

"From the first hours, I was very much impressed with the performance of the Canadian Despatch Riders—the skill they showed, and the speed! We [the Dutch people] were always astonished by the very characteristic manner in which the Canadian DRs rode, straight upright, sitting on the petrol tank, with sometimes two or three passengers [usually Dutch girls!] behind. No one could tell me why it was done so. The British didn't ride that way. Somebody guessed that they could handle their machines more easily, but I tried it and did not see that. Perhaps it was just for show. If so, they had great success. The elderly people still talk about it!"

Command did everything within its power to discourage this bizarre practice. At home and overseas, Part I Orders listed almost daily reminders addressed specifically to delinquent riders, threatening disciplinary action for a variety of misdemeanours, all of which the riders universally ignored following a brief token period of good behaviour.

> Part I Orders, Item 275, Discipline, Improvised Seats M/C: The procedure of operating m/cs from an improvised seat of rubber or a folded blanket strapped to the petrol tank forward of the saddle is on the increase. The m/c [lightweight] is scientifically designed by the manufacturer to WD specifications and no departure from the correct riding position is to be permitted. This practice will cease as of the publication of this order. Provosts have been instructed to charge offenders and confiscate any improvised seats set forward of the standard saddle.

There were lesser offenses listed too, like "driving mirrors in use as shaving mirrors, m/c pillion seats as pillows, mattresses or office cushions, strips of inner tubes lashed to frames to make a bed, and windscreens in use as office tables," but the big problem was, not surprisingly, speeding:

> October, 1940: To force drivers of m/cs to realize their responsibilities, the following maximum speed limits are ordered forthwith in the area [Aldershot, Farnham, Sandhurst]: 30 mph. A competent motorcyclist will have an accurate idea of 30 mph without a speedometer.

Naturally, not much attention was paid to this limit, so a few months later, speed limit stickers were issued to be placed on motorcycles. The success of this venture can be judged by the Part I Orders that followed: "Recent checks of military vehicles reveal that officers, warrant officers, NCOs and drivers, especially of m/cs, continue to display an irresponsible disregard of the speed regulations as laid down."

**An improvised seat set forward of the standard saddle adorns this 16H of the 2nd LAA Regiment, RCA.**

# PTE VIC HAUGHEY

## 23rd Field Company, RCE

"I enlisted on Saturday, the day before war was declared. I was sent to depot, then to Halifax, and then to Camp Petawawa." It was at Petawawa that Haughey rode his first motorcycle, an Indian. When he joined the 23rd Field Company, RCE, 1st Army Troops, he moved to Sussex, New Brunswick, and was issued a Harley, "a good machine and heavy."

Upon arriving in England, Haughey asked to be demoted. "I said I would revert if I could become a DR. I got my Harley, took off the windshield (hard on the face when hill climbing) and the pillion seat. If I had to take someone with me, they rode on the rider's seat and I rode on the tank." The removal of the pillion seat discouraged officers from requesting a ride as well as making the offering of a ride optional.

"The Harley could take a lot of punishment, especially on convoys, as long as you kept it in good shape. Hill climbing, however, was another story. Grassy hills in dry weather were fine, but in the rain? We started training and had to make that hill no matter what, then move onto the next one, which was much worse, then into the gravel pits, down one side and up the other."

As D-Day approached, Haughey was given a Matchless, "a good bike on hills and much lighter to pick up than the Harley, but on hard convoy work, I had to put in an exhaust valve after every convoy of thirty-two trucks."

Keeping convoy vehicles evenly spaced was a problem for DRs on escort duty; too close, and accidents happened; strung out too far, the length of the line became unmanageable, increasing the risk of losing vehicles at intersections. "We were like mother hens

**Above: Matchless GL3.**

to the convoy, taking messages back and forth while moving, checking tires, trailer hitches, and tarps, and reporting to the front end.

"Someone from another unit would get in your convoy, and when they got out, you had to close up the gap. I had one driver whom I relied on, a chap named Hubbard from Nova Scotia. He drove a White scout armoured car, half-inch steel on the front, a quarter inch on the sides. When an unwanted person got in on us, I would ride up and ask them very politely to leave. If they didn't, I dropped back and got Hubbard. He just bounced them out. No problem.

"The Normandy, France, area was rough on DRs—dry, dusty, and hot. Dust and convoys brought on the enemy's ME 109. They loved convoys, so if possible, we travelled at night, which was more dangerous for the DR.

"The worst part was carrying messages at night. You couldn't shine a light to see the map, so you had to remember landmarks, or what was left of them. One wrong turn could mean the enemy had you and a Matchless.

"One night, one of our drivers had an attack of appendicitis. We were too far from a hospital, so the transportation sergeant suggested we take him to the nearest town and get a doctor. We bundled him up into the jeep, I got on my bike (it was pitch black), and eventually we found the doctor. He answered the door, rushed us down into the cellar, and then said, 'Now go!' We told the doctor we would be back in the morning. The next day, heading for town, we were stopped by one of the guys on our side. He asked us where we thought we were going. We told him. He said, 'As soon as we take the town you can go in and get your man.' The enemy had occupied the town the night before! We waited the morning and went and got him out. A day in the life of a DR.

"The enemy didn't like DRs. They used to snipe at us from church towers, tall buildings, etc. I think we got used to being shot at."

The longest ride for Haughey was from St. Omer, France, to Nijmegen, Holland. Both food and sleep were scarce. And meals were served cold as there was not enough time to pause for cooking. "Paratroopers were going to be dropped at Arnhem, and they needed us to carry assault troops over the Waal River to back them up. We left 16 September 1944. All traffic was waved off so we could go flat out." When they arrived, their assault role became an evacuation role. "On the night of 25 September we brought out 2,500 1st British Airborne out of 2,800. I lost one truck, hit going in for the second time as it neared the Nijmegen Bridge. We were attached to the 30th British Corps and got no recognition for our efforts, but we know what we did."

In Holland, Haughey found conditions to be quite different from Normandy. "We went to bed, if you could call it that, wet and tired. The next day, we were at it again. Wake up, put on a pair of frozen boots and your still-wet clothes. We had one thought in mind-home-and that's what kept us going."

Holland was crisscrossed by canals, each having to be crossed before the Canadians could advance. Getting boats into the water without the enemy noticing was difficult and dangerous. "We would drive along the dyke roads at night without any lights on. A DR would walk ahead of each truck carrying a sign about fourteen by fourteen behind his back. One side was black, the other side fluorescent. When the truck ahead stopped, the DR would turn the sign to black and pray that the truck behind would stop. We did a lot of praying in those days."

Haughey was in Nordhorn, Germany, when the enemy surrendered. "We moved back to the Almelo area. I got a BSA and rode it to Enschede with a message. It went into a speed wobble on the way there, but I got out of it. On the way back, carrying another

**A heavy work load meant that DRs often had to catch a nap where and when possible. Pte L. Wilkins of the Essex Regiment grabs a few winks and a cigar at Arnhem, Netherlands, 14 April 1945. The paint worn off the rear of the gas tank of this BSA M20 was a by-product of the prohibited Canadian riding position (seated upon the tank). The bullet hole gracing the toolbox was a by-product of the enemy attempting to put an end to this bizarre practice.**

message, it started shimmying again. This time I could do nothing but ride it down, which I did on about fifty yards of pavement." When Haughey got back to camp, he found out that the message he had been carrying, and sliding along the pavement with, had his name on it. He was being shipped back to Winnipeg. "The medic patched me up, and I suffered until I was about halfway home."

**CTS instructor Capt Jerry Bradshaw on a Harley-Davidson leads a student on a Norton through a water crossing at Lindford Ford, Hampshire, England, 14 October 1942.**

While in England, it was not unusual for Canadian DR units to challenge British units to cross-country duels. At first, the British thought this would be like taking candy from a baby. One account, from a British DR's point of view, observed "when it came to the high-speed bit they left us standing. Sitting right up forward on the tank in their usual way, they just bulldozed their way through, ignoring ruts and water holes. We had never seen anything like it."[27]

Nor had the British heard much like it. In August of 1942, a Battalion Order was issued: "DRs will not cause excessive noise by causing their machines to backfire." The effect on the British public of these explosions while a war was on was interesting to say the least. Another order during the same month read: "All ranks are warned that pillion riding is forbidden." And the month prior, orders were issued that "The practice of removing toilet paper from latrines must cease immediately." Perhaps it comes as no surprise then that the title Crazy Canucks was soon bestowed upon motorcycle-mounted Canadians.

**Crazy Canucks Steve Berezowsuti, Jim Ercolini, Dan Daily and Bill Gunning.**

**Ray Lehman forces a Harley-Davidson through the mud of a cold British winter.**

This well-deserved reputation did not go unnoticed by the enemy either. Lord Haw Haw, the Nazi radio announcer, was reported to have said that the Canadian soldier did not worry the Axis-aligned nations as they knew how to deal with the rebellious lot. "Just give them a bottle of whisky and a motorcycle and they will kill themselves."

Canadian riders vehemently disputed that claim. They knew the vile English weather would get them first. Not since 1894 had Britain experienced a winter as cold as the one that welcomed the first boatloads of Canadian troops in 1939, and the winters of 1940-1942 were not any better. The War Diary for D Company, 2nd Canadian Pioneer, RCE, CASF, observed on 4 November 1940, "Rain continuous—mud conditions very bad" and on the eleventh, "Steady rain, progress in training discouraging as it is impossible to carry on any recreational program." One word described the thirteenth: "Snow."

Often billeted in tents, the riders found the incessant rain, wet snow and fog prevented anything from drying out. Despite the conditions, they were not permitted to "wear gum boots or boots, knee, rubber."

Combined with shortages of virtually everything, officers were faced with a morale problem. "CO of A Company advised wine cellar in his billets broken into and looted by troops—matter being investigated." Yet somehow, amid the pouring rain, the troops were organized into "a highly mobile, quick acting, hard hitting reserve"[28] whose primary objective was the defence of England.

A key instrument in this mobility was the Norton Big 4. The armoured sidecar unit was fitted with a Bren gun and served in lieu of the scarce heavier mobile artillery, operating in unison with fast-moving columns. A typical reconnaissance squadron of the time ideally consisted of one officer's motorcycle with sidecar and driver, twelve Norton Big 4s, each with a driver, gunner and extra man riding pillion, a sergeant and two DRs on solo machines and a 15-cwt truck with driver. As more equipment became available, all but the motorcycles of the two DRs were exchanged for armoured vehicles, the Big 4s then used for normal motorcycle duties in England away from any potential combat area.

Aldershot in the south of England became the focal point of Canadian activities, and was soon overcrowded with soldiers wallowing in the mud. The billets were small brick and stone buildings, each identical, each possessing antiquated plumbing and heating systems, and no insulation. And the training, like the rain, never seemed to stop. More rubber boots and raincoats were needed than existed in England.

The little transport available was in constant use. Workshops, like the one at Bordon, Hampshire, run by the RCEME, were burdened with a backlog of rebuilds. Breakdowns

**A column of Canadians on patrol near Aldershot, England, 14 December 1940. The Norton Big 4s are accompanied by solo riders on Norton 16Hs.**

occurred daily, and maintenance, because of the weather, was minimal. In order to maintain battle readiness, a Motor Transit Holiday was declared for each Monday: "On this day, all MT (including m/cs) in the Canadian Corps other than that required for essential services will be taken off the road and the day will be devoted to unit inspection and maintenance." Even without the necessary spare parts and tires, this holiday did help to keep the bikes on the road.

To preserve the motorcycles for official use, CMHQ attempted to curtail riding through the issuance of mandatory work tickets:

> Use of Motorcycles: Duty calls for m/cs to go to Signal Sgt for allotment of m/c and making out of Work Tickets. Signal Sgt to see that rider has an AFA 2038 and has passed test as m/c rider. Motorcycles are not in good shape and are to be used only for Despatch riding and training, the training to be done under the supervision of Signal Corporal or his representative. Daily Work Tickets are required for each m/c and each and every trip must be recorded on the Work Ticket the same as for trucks. All recreational journeys of over 40 miles total distance to be investigated by Coy commanders and reported to the CO, the Transport office to report such journeys to the Coy commanders.

Riding in England presented many new challenges for Canadian motorcyclists, the most obvious being navigation of the narrow, busy roads on the "wrong" side. Even if a rider were to master this feat with minimal fuss, there was no guarantee that he might not meet a truck or tank driver coming around a corner who had not yet adjusted to the change.

Traffic accidents were a common problem and the issue made regular appearances in Part I Orders. "In a large proportion of the accidents reported to this HQ, the evidence reveals that the driver concerned had been following another vehicle at too close an interval. The prevalence of this practice, especially among DRs, has been confirmed by actual observation." Also, bicycles and motorcycles were being forced into ditches by the wide swoops that transport drivers made turning onto sideroads.

> Nov 6, 1941: Road accidents—There are no messages being sent at the present time that are so urgent that a DR should feel obligated to run unnecessary risks. (Maj-Gen G. R. Pearkes).
>
> Dec 1, 1942: A number of serious accidents, one of which was fatal, have recently resulted from jiffy stands, both on Harley-Davidson and Norton m/cs, coming down when in motion. All m/cs will be checked to ensure that the springs for holding jiffy stands in place are sufficiently strong to prevent them from shaking loose when on the road. In the case of Nortons, it might be necessary to wire up the stands permanently.
>
> May 15, 1943: Gnr Phillips G. S. of the 52nd Battery decided to learn to ride a motorcycle and was taken to Brecon hospital with a broken leg.
>
> July 5, 1941: Motorcyclists when in movement will NOT salute.

**A Norton 16H gets attention from Corporal Smith of the Royal Montreal Regiment, with help from a DR of the Canadian Forestry Corps, at Bordon, Hampshire, England, 1 May 1942.**

**Ruth Cameron and her Harley-Davidson on Vancouver Island, BC, during the summer of 1944.**

Traffic accidents were not the only hazard in England. On 6 July 1940 three RCOC soldiers at Aldershot were killed in a bombing raid while servicing motorcycle sidecar units for the reconnaissance squadrons. They were the first Canadian soldiers to die from enemy attack on English soil.

Because of a motorcycle's engine noise, riders were unable to hear the air-raid sirens while out on their bikes, so when they saw the locals run for shelter, the DR either joined them or raced out of the vicinity at top speed.

> Nov 4, 1942: Picture on VD shown to all ranks.
>
> Dec 7,1942: M/c backfired and burned on the way between Bn HQ and B Coy while on DRLS.
>
> Dec 23, 1942, just in time for Christmas: Prophylactic station opened at #6 Gas Clearing Stn, at Penholme, Dorking.

Unlike England's large populace of military riders, Canadian DRs were all male. In England, the Auxiliary Transport Service (ATS) and the Women's Royal Navy Service (WRNS, or Wrens) both used female DRs extensively for escorts and delivering messages. They rode the same long hours, over the same poor roads and through the same abusive weather conditions as their male counterparts did within any Allied force stationed in Britain.

Ruth Cameron was a Canadian motorcyclist who wanted to serve her country doing what she knew best—riding a motorcycle. At age twenty-five, she joined the Canadian Women's Army Corps (CWAC) with the understanding that, yes, it would be possible. Once she was enlisted, however, the army said no. An effort was even made to prevent her from riding her own bike during off-duty hours.

A small number of women did receive motorcycle riding lessons at Barriefield, but none rode in active service, so the purpose of the training remains a mystery. It is a shame that somewhere in the massive mechanism of Canada's war effort, enthusiasm like Ruth Cameron's could not have found an outlet. The loss was obviously Canada's as much as Ruth's.

Prior to the invasion of Europe, it was the continuing series of exercises that posed the greatest danger to a rider. Exercises were mock battles designed to acquaint all levels of the forces with the extreme difficulty of moving great quantities of equipment and men over vast distances. England was defended and Europe invaded countless times without any soldiers ever leaving Britain or meeting the enemy.

Each exercise was given a code name, like Hare, Waterloo, Beaver, Tiger, Blackboy,

**DRs of the 48th Highlanders of Canada prepare for their day's work.**

Spartan, Grizzly, Pickaxe or Harlequin. Fox was the first, held in February of 1941. It ended in a monumental traffic jam. But by October of that year, over a quarter of a million troops had successfully been moved across England in exercise Bumper.

At the centre of each exercise was the motorcyclist, directing traffic, manning road blocks, acting as umpires, delivering urgent messages and supplies and keeping convoys together and moving, regardless of weather conditions or time of day: "Sept 25, 1941: DRs getting busier all the time; phones ringing, messages being written, cancelled, rewritten."

Upon the completion of Bumper, Lt-Col G. C. McArthur, C.R., RCASC, 1st Canadian Division, issued a letter lauding the services rendered by the DRs during the exercise.

The following outline of a DR's responsibilities for Spartan was typical of what might be expected of a rider:

> The leading vehicle of each block of vehicles will use sidelights and the rear vehicle will use tail lights. All other vehicles will be restricted to rear axle lighting only. All units will maintain DR communication with HQ. The Coy will require 10 DRs, therefore two each will be attached from 505 and 506 Fd Coys.
>
> One DR at all times at Btn HQ. When a DR is despatched, a replacement must be sent.
>
> Task: Seize and occupy capital of England—Huntingdon (forces roughly equal). Simultaneous sea force invasion of east coast from North Sea.
>
> Movement and traffic control: 30 vehicles/mile by day, 40 by night.

**A convoy at rest during an exercise somewhere in England. The five motorcycles are all Norton 16Hs.**

> Speed: 15 mph by day, 7 1/2 mph by night.
>
> Halts: 10 minutes to every even clock hour, normal maintenance on halts. All convoys pull off to the side of the road to allow priority convoys through. No smoking at night. All movements other than essential will be done at night. Daylight moves not more than eight vehicles per block.

It was the DR's job to ensure that these orders were carried out. Riders landing on the east coast were required to load and unload their motorcycles from landing craft. Immediately after Spartan, one War Diary proudly boasted of having the "first decent bath in two weeks."

The risks to the riders on exercises were immense. It was acknowledged that a rider on convoy duty could not accomplish his job if he stuck to the speed limits as ordered. Generally, the practice was for one rider to man an intersection to ensure convoy vehicles proceeded in the intended direction while another, if available, would run up and down the convoy, keeping the convoy moving to prevent stragglers from getting lost. Should a vehicle break down, the rider would make note of its position and report it to the Light Aid Detachment (LAD).

It was not unusual for a rider to reach speeds of up to sixty-five miles per hour, weaving between tanks, half-tracks and supply trucks travelling in either direction. And, while racing around the convoy, he was also expected to watch for poor road conditions, evidence of enemy action, broken communication lines, units that had moved into or out of an area, and anything that might be the least bit suspicious.

Only the absence of gunfire aimed in their direction made exercises any less hazardous than real war. Riding at night with no useful lighting, through rain and fog, unseen by the other vehicles also travelling without lights, struggling to get a bike ashore in high waves, the rider sometimes going without sleep for forty-eight hours straight—casualties were the expected and unavoidable price of preparing for direct confrontation.

# CPL LENO CARON, CPL CONRADE NELSON, AND SGT MORLEY YOUNG

2nd RCCS

Leno Caron and Conrade Nelson were both DRs in the 2nd RCCS, 6 DR Section. Morley Young served as the senior NCO in 6 DR Section, and on 10 July 1944 was cross-posted to 5 DR Section. Five DR Section operated out of Corps and advanced Corps HQ, and often called upon members of 6 DR Section in rear HQ for reinforcements, or when additional DRs were required for particular operations. What follows are the individual stories of Caron, Nelson and Young, their shared and separate experiences tending to weave together like the strings of a loose macramé, distinct, yet each definitely part of a total fabric. With additional notes taken from official war diaries, it becomes a fascinating look into the life of a DR; a glimpse of wartime friendships, adventure, comedy, and tragedy.

Nelson: "Signalman Curran had been on SDR duty at the Dover Castle signal office when he was informed he was being sent to the Normandy beaches. As I was told, he was riding back to camp, about seven miles, to pick up his gear before heading down to the docks and must have been highly elated at being the first in our unit to cross the channel. He was travelling at top speed."

Caron: "Signalman W. F. Curran was a very good friend of mine. We all called him Dick. For a while in England, I'd say four or five months, Dick and I were personal DRs for Gen Guy Simonds.

**Above: Morley Young at Barriefield, Kingston, Ontario, 1940.**

"Dick was killed in England on the night of 5-6 June 1944. He and I were on twelve-hour duty as SDRs. I was on day shift, Dick on nights.

"On SDR, you were on standby to take out only top priority messages. We were stationed in Dover, and Dick had to make a run to Portsmouth. On his way back, just a few miles from camp, he drifted over to the right-hand side of the road into the path of a three-ton lorry. The truck driver tried to avoid him by turning into the embankment on the roadside, but the nose dug in and the truck spun around, killing him."

The value of war can be measured in dollars spent, territories gained or lost and treaties signed, but it can never be measured in friends lost.

Nelson: "Corporal Shirlow and I made a pact at Three Bridges in England. Whichever of us woke up first would wake the other. Then we would quietly wash, shave, make our beds, get dressed, and, last of all, get out our stiff brushes and make a real noise polishing our boots. This would wake up the rest of the nuts and bring down a barrage of curses and flying objects upon us. Shirlow would laugh like mad."

Caron: "Sergeant Hannay and I'm sure it was Corporal Shirlow were killed when they drove their jeep into a mine field."

Nelson: "It was the cook's afternoon off and they decided to visit Caen, but activity there was still too fierce so Shirlow turned the jeep around to go back. One front wheel went off the road on to the sand where an enemy Tellermine was hidden and the cook and Shirlow were killed. Fortunately, the signalman driver who was sitting in the back of the jeep was blown out backwards and only suffered bruises."

Young: "Sergeant Hannay and Corporal Shirlow were in 5 DR section with me. They lost their lives at Buron, between Caen and the beachhead on 13 July 1944."

Nelson: "We buried Corporal Shirlow in a temporary cemetery beside our camp."

The 6 DR Section landed in France 1 July 1944, after having become separated from the main body of the 2nd RCCS on the way over. For five days, they lived off their ration packs until the cook and his truck caught up with them.

Nelson: "During our first two weeks in Normandy, I had to make a short trip of about five miles, twice a day, over to a little town. I travelled at the regulation forty miles per hour, which isn't fast and isn't slow, and makes it very hard for a rifleman to judge his lead-off, especially if there is a breeze.

"About halfway to the town, there was a church with a square tower and imitation battlements on the roof of the tower. It sat back in a field with a dirt path leading up to it from the road."

Every time Nelson rode by the church, he heard a buzzing sound, which he put down to "those damn little wasps that infested Normandy by the millions." It wasn't until he heard a "chirp" in his ear that he realized he was being sniped at and that the sniper was beginning to "learn my speed. I didn't get scared—I got mad as hell, because, not being John Wayne, I couldn't fire back from my bike with a Sten gun."

When he got to town this time, he reported the incident to "a cluster of infantry. The Sarge and a few of his men went out into the field and made an elaborate show of setting up and aiming a mortar into the church. In a few moments, a German soldier came running out of the church door with his hands in the air."

It also was about this time that Nelson "clobbered my first bike." He had got a message to deliver at 2100 hours, 16 July 1944. He had just left the light of the Signal Office tent, his eyes not yet accustomed to the dark of the night, when he spotted an English DR scooting by. "I decided to follow his red tail-light until my eyes adjusted. He turned left at the first crossroad—just the way I was going."

**Conrade Nelson with No. 6 DR Section, RCCS, in England.**

Nelson turned too, but the red light was gone. "Instead, I saw a little white light on my left, and a little white light on my right. Instantly, I rolled backwards off my bike and let it go. There was a dull thump and a clang or two."

When he picked himself up and walked forward, he found the remains of his bike stuffed into the front of an English armoured car. Fellow Signalman Burtch had to deliver the message that night.

The 22 July was overcast and raining, turning the roads to mud. All motorcycles were taken off the road for the day.

Nelson remembers Caron very well: "very humorous at times and easy going. He was with 5 DR Section when they were parked in an apple orchard on the north side of Caen and the German mortars zeroed in on them. Most of their motorcycles were knocked out but they received brand-new bikes the next day, which says something good for the RCASC."

Caron: "Whenever we moved camp, two of my fellow DRs, Corporal Lush and Signalman Horton, would always dig a foxhole about five- or six-feet deep. I would watch, and then dig my hole about a foot deep right near them. When the shelling started and things got too hot, I would jump into their hole. They would curse me and tell me to dig my own hole and I'd say, 'Yes, yes, but wait till things cool down.' Of course, when the shelling stopped, I didn't need a deep hole. This went on all across France."

Caron was proud of his Norton: "When we turned in our Harleys for Nortons before D-Day (we were given English machines because we could load one on each jeep for landing in France), I removed the Harley's windshield and lap apron and installed them on the Norton. I was the only rider that had a Norton with a windshield."

Shortly after landing in France, Caron was on a run near Camilly. Both sides of the road were lined with people coming toward him, returning to what was left of their homes, or fleeing from the front. Suddenly, they all started running into the fields: "I thought I must be awful tough-looking to scare all these people!" Caron was unaware of the enemy ME109 fighter aircraft strafing the road behind him until "the road started jumping apart in front and beside me. I was in the ditch in a flash scratching for cover.

A week or so later near the village of Lasson, I was on another DR run when six fighter planes come in strafing the road and everything in the general area." Caron leapt off his bike and was running for a slit trench when a soldier in the trench called out a warning to be careful of the mines. "I had no time to be careful. It was a choice of being shot or blown up. I just kept going and made it to the trench."

From there, Caron and the other soldier had a ringside seat to a full aerial dogfight as a group of RAF fighters attacked the enemy. "Bullets were coming down like rain.

**Mud was a continuous problem for motorcyclists. Note the bouquet of flowers carried by the leading Provost, attached to the handlebars of his BSA. The trailing Provost has a map secured to the bars of his Norton. Both items were rare, non-military issue add-ons.**

Four enemy planes were shot down. I escaped unhurt."

Nelson: "We did get strafed once in a while, even up in the Reichswald, by Messerschmidts, but the pilots were very young, even compared to us. They made serious mistakes. They would fly lengthways down a convoy from the rear at only about tree-top level. Being this low, the bullets from the wing guns would straddle the road, missing the vehicles altogether. Fifty feet higher up, and the cones of fire from their guns would have met right on the trucks."

Caron: "Second Corps later moved on through the city of Caen. We set-up camp at Hubert Folie, near a place called Verriers, on 8 August. The enemy must have spotted us moving in, because for five days until we moved forward to get away from it, we were shelled at least four to five times a day. It seemed that every time we came to camp for meal or rest, they would cut loose at us with their 88s.

**Leno Caron with a Sten gun at Cairon, France. The ammunition belt and dagger are both ex-German. Note the Harley-Davidson windshield on his Norton.**

"When we pulled into the camp area, about twelve riders parked in a group and started walking toward the kitchen truck about 150 feet away. An enemy 88 artillery shell landed on our bikes. We lost eight machines, the kitchen truck was punched full of shrapnel holes, and two of our DRs were hit. Signalman Meyers got a bad head wound and died a few weeks later in hospital. Sergeant Young was cut on the head by shrapnel, and just needed first aid. He died later in Holland in a traffic accident." (See below.)

Young: "DRs in my section travelled anywhere from four to seven thousand miles per week, and not without severe casualties. A total of fifty-two DRs passed through the section during this period, but we were rarely ever up to full strength of thirty-five."

Young's official diary covering the operation of 5 DR Section for the period of July 1944 to January 1945 records six DRs killed in action and four seriously wounded. Still others were injured in accidents requiring varying periods of hospitalization. Contrary to Caron's report, Young was not among the deceased.

"I was first wounded outside of Caen on the road to Falaise at the village of Hubert Folie. A direct 88 fell or hit on the DR lines, wounding Signalman Nuite and myself. He was seriously wounded behind the ear and had to be evacuated, but lived and returned to join the section later in Holland. I was patched up at the regimental aid post and kept on going.

"When the shell dropped, it fell over Corporal Lush's head and exploded directly in front of us. Had it fallen six feet shorter, we would have all been gone.

"Prior to this, another shell had fallen and seriously wounded A. P. Meyers and F. J. Wright." Meyers died of his injuries, while Wright rejoined the section later.

Another shelling, 11 August, saw Corporal Lush receive minor injuries to the cheek and two motorcycles badly damaged. Signalman Nelson reported getting a puncture.

On the 5 September, 2nd RCCS were on the move from Moyenneville to Montreuil. While travelling east of Montreuil, Young entered a small village near Hesdin. To his surprise, he and the other Canadians with him were the first liberators to reach the area. Parked in the village square, he heard someone call "Hi! You Canucks!" The voice was that of an American airman.

"He, Bill Waddell of Pennsylvania, had bailed out three months prior with the rest of his B-17 crew, and since then, had been concealed by the men and women of the French underground. During the day, the Americans hid in a hollowed-out bakery woodpile. The entrance was under the cobblestones of the bakery yard. At night, they would take refuge in several houses in the nearby vicinity."

Young delivered a happy Waddell and his crew to HQ the next day, who in turn sent them on to freedom. "I wrote to Waddell's parents to tell them he was alive, free, and that he would contact them later after debriefing, etc. Bill died in 1982, but I still keep in touch with the family."

Nelson: "Our company moved across the Seine at Rouen. Signalman Burtch and I went ahead about a half a mile to scout the road in case of impediments. We were riding side by side. The road started to turn and climb steeply up a hill to a town that looked positively medieval to me. It was closed in by a high brick wall. We had to gear down to second as we reached the top, then the road curved left through an arch in the wall. On the other side, we saw a crowd of waving, cheering, yelling townspeople. They were massed in a straight line to our right clean across to the other arch on the opposite side of town. Behind them, were the narrow streets and houses of the town. We stopped, side by side, and just sat there being applauded.

"As we had come through the arch, I had seen the tail end of an enemy convoy going out the other gate. The last vehicle was a jeep-type almost impossibly loaded with household stuff, like tables, mattresses, etc.

"Our colonel's jeep was next through the arch, followed by the trucks. Burtch had got a redhead girl on the back of his bike and was riding back and forth across the square. I wheeled over to Colonel North's jeep and reported that I had seen the enemy garrison racing out of here, but he seemed unconcerned."

That night, they set up camp just a few miles out of town.

"The tarps were spread out from the signal trucks to form a couple of offices, but none of the operators or DRs set up their sleeping tents because that was to be only an overnight stop. Sergeant Vezina detailed roving pickets for the night and we made our beds (sacks) near a five-foot high wall.

"Early in the morning, I was shaken awake. 'Come on, wake up. Wake up the others, but keep quiet.' I could see people rushing quietly back and forth, and heard the sergeant-major say to one of the operators, 'Never mind rolling up the wires, we haven't time. Just cut 'em and leave 'em.'

"I asked what was up while I was rolling up my bedroll. The colonel had got a message for us to go back. We were ten miles into enemy territory!

"Signalman Paquette and I followed the last truck out on to the road. As we were going out, I looked back over the wall. Going out the gate of the opposite field was the tail end of the enemy convoy. They were getting out just as fast as we were. 'If we had been on our toes,' I said to Paquette, 'we could have taken them without a shot.'

"Paquette said, 'No, no. We've got a million dollars in radio equipment in the ACVs [Armoured Communication Vehicles]. The officers couldn't risk it.'

"Johnny Paquette was the guy who, one icy day, had his throttle cable break, so he wrapped the cable around a piece of branch like a handle and was tearing down the road all day manipulating the throttle by tugging on that piece of wood while steering with

**DR Arnold Burtch arrives on time. Second World War military censors have retouched the photograph to remove the unit markings from the Norton's front fender, a standard practice for pictures slated for publication.**

the other hand on almost glare ice!"

Caron: "While we were in Belgium stationed near the city of Ghent, we made runs toward Zeebruge on the coast, and to units in the area of the Leopold Canal. The trouble with this was our troops held one side of the canal, and the enemy the other. The shortest route was along the canal, so that's the way we went.

"I would lay down on the tank of my Norton and as far over the side as I could, holding the throttle wide open. That would be about seventy miles per hour on a good day. The enemy would fire at us from across the canal as we rode by like ducks in a shooting gallery."

In November 1944, 5 DR section moved from Ghent, Belgium, into Holland, arriving at the village of Wijchen (between Grave and Nijmegen) on the ninth of that month (the previous night, they had "slept out in the mud"). The advance had come to a stop, but DR duties continued, maintaining communications across the many river areas to the frontline troops, despite the cold, rain, snow, slippery roads and unrelenting enemy fire.

Young: "Obviously, I did not lose my life in the Netherlands, but was wounded and evacuated to Belgium, and then to England. This happened in early February during operation Veritable and my war was over. I was in hospital for many months."

Caron: "You tell me Sergeant Young is alive and I seen him lying dead!

"We were living behind a convent in a stable. That's what we called home. It was in a small graveyard. I don't recall what month it was, but a DR came in and said Sergeant Young was killed in an accident. I and another DR took a jeep to see for ourselves.

"In the area of the accident, we asked where the sergeant was, and were led into a building that may have been an office of some kind in peacetime. Young was lying on his back upon a table or desk." An officer, whom Caron presumed to be a doctor, came in and "looked Young over, then declared, 'This man is dead. Send him to the morgue.' That's the last I saw of Sergeant Young."

Young: "There was a building at the crossroads on the Grave-Nijmegen road, used as a casualty clearing station, and here is where I believe Caron saw me. In early February, I was badly wounded in the area east of Nijmegen, on the road to Cleve, and was brought back by jeep ambulance to be placed on a Dakota aircraft at the Grave airport for evacuation to England. En route, I believe I passed through that CCS. However, I was out at the time. This is the only possible explanation I have. It must be so, because I am alive!"

After Young's departure from 5 DR section, Corporal Lush was promoted to lance sergeant, and on 20 March 1945 was posted to 6 DR section.

Because of the potentially dire consequences that could result from an official war diary falling into enemy hands, the diaries were not intended to be detailed sources of useful information on the war itself. Instead, each diary abounds in trivia. For instance, 5 DR Section diary records that during the month of April 1945 the section's one jeep, two Humbers, and sixteen motorcycles covered a total of 57,940 miles. It also notes that Caron and Horton went on leave to England on the fifth of the same month, and returned on the seventeenth.

The diary for 6 DR Section shows that throughout the conflict, various charges were laid against the men serving this section for speeding, dangerous driving, improper lighting on a vehicle, poor maintenance, and for "not getting up when called."

Nelson: "Winter in Holland can be as cold, bleak and miserable as any experienced in Canada. It was on such a day in January 1945, having just finished a run into Nijmegen and returned with the messages I picked up, that I received a special request.

"Our unit was housed for the winter in a convent about five miles west of Nijmegen. I went in the side door near the end of the building, down the stairs, and through another door into the Signal Office. The basement was the best place for the Signal Office because every night starting about 2300 hrs, the buzz bombs started flying right over the roof on their way to Antwerp.

"I handed my packets to the DR clerk along with the message receipts. Then the Operating Section Corporal walked over to me and said, 'Nelson, we have an urgent SDR message that must go out right away. Will you take it?' I said something like, 'If it's gotta go, it's gotta go. Where to?'

"The whole Signal Office fell sort of quiet. No one spoke. Everybody looked at us very seriously. I got an ominous prickly feeling all over.

"The Corporal showed me over to the map wall, the Lance Corporal easing in beside us as my attention was directed to a pin on the map. A little rectangular paper flag representing a Division HQ was pasted near the top of the pin. Nothing unusual about that. The map was covered with such pin-flags. The appalling thing was that this flag was that of a German armoured division, spotted about ten miles north of the Arnhem Bridge, well into enemy territory.

"'You are to take this envelope over to the General there. He has radioed us that he wants to surrender his division and wants to know the procedure for doing so. When he has read this he will either give you a reply to bring back or he and some of his officers will ask you to escort them back here.'

"'You gotta be kidding! You're pulling my leg!'"

"'It's orders,' the Corporal insisted. 'Will you go or do I have to call your Sergeant and get someone else?'

"In our outfit, to turn down a request to go on a run, especially an SDR, was considered to be humiliating because we thought it indicated that you were scared and willing to put another DR at risk. 'If that's the order, of course I'll go, but look at that map. I'll ride into Nijmegen, turn right and over the Nijmegen Bridge, crossing the Waal, and make it to the south end of the Arnhem Bridge. I know there is at least one of our tank units on the land between the bridges.'

"'So what's the problem?' asked the Corporal.

"Exasperated, I sputtered, 'As soon as I come over the crest of the Arnhem Bridge, the Germans will spot me. There's a huge concrete bunker overlooking the north end. They'll machine gun me down as soon as I'm in range and all I've got is a Browning pistol!'

"'Oh, don't worry about that, the Krauts at the other end of the bridge know you're coming. And besides, we'll give you a white flag to put on your bike.'

"'A fat lot of good that will do. What about all the Krauts between there and Division HQ?'

"The Corporal appeared to be getting irritated, passing off my objections with 'When you get to the end of the bridge, they'll probably give you an escort and all that stuff.'

"Turning toward the door in a very unpleasant mood, I stuffed the message into my shoulder bag. Johnny Paquette, who had come in after me and overheard the latter half of the conversation, said, 'I'll go with you.' It really shook me, having a friend that would do a thing like that.

"'No, no,' I said, 'There's no use two of us becoming POWs, if not dead.'

"I started for the door, convinced it was all over for me. I was just turning the handle when suddenly the Corporal hollered 'Nelson! It's just a gag. Go get your supper.' The whole Signal Office burst out laughing. What a superb bunch of actors—the CBC could sure use them.

"I stood there frozen for a moment, then, when I recovered, I said, 'YOU ROTTEN BUNCH OF ^@@##!!*, I'll get you for this!' Another chorus of raucous laughter, and I turned and stomped out the door thinking they must have planned this for an hour at least. That's the trouble with non-coms; always horsing around."

Caron: "A DR was shot in the foot by a fellow DR. But he was happy! His wife in England was expecting a baby soon, and this was his ticket to get back to see her."

Such accidents were not rare. On 18 December 1944 Signalman Wilks was accidentally shot and critically wounded, and on 6 January 1945 Caron attended the court martial of the soldier involved, who was found guilty of negligence. Caron was also almost shot himself.

"In our winter home, there was a ground floor and an attic. I was sitting on a stretcher we used for a bed on the ground floor, when a DR in the attic accidentally fired his pistol. The shot came through the attic floor and into the stretcher, missing my right side by inches.

"All this accidental shooting was with Browning automatic pistols. At first, we were issued Sten guns, but the DRs didn't want to carry them because sometimes when you hit a bump, the Sten gun would fire." So the Sten guns were replaced with Browning pistols.

"The pistols were nice guns, but when you cleaned them, or cocked them, or fired the last shell in the clip, the action stayed open. When a full clip was put in, the action closed with a shell in the barrel and the hammer cocked, all set to fire. Then, you would put your thumb on the hammer, pull the trigger and let the hammer down slow and put the safety on. Sometimes, men would forget to hold the hammer, pull the trigger, and someone was injured or killed."

As a senior NCO for both 5 and 6 DR Sections, it seems appropriate that Sergeant Young should have the last word in this brief look into the two Signal Corps sections. "I am proud to have served this country in war, and particularly to have been a member of the RCCS. I have many fond memories of the DRs. They were tops!"[29]

Initial encounters with the enemy, for example at Hong Kong, were poorly planned and executed. Dieppe was a classic, sombre illustration of this ineptitude, one which no rationalization could justify. Of the 6,000 troops that landed on the beaches around Dieppe, 4,963 were Canadians. They landed at dawn, 19 August 1942. The enemy was ready and waiting. At 9 a.m., with the troops pinned down and bleeding on the beaches, the order was given to withdraw. By 2 p.m., it was all over. Only 2,210 returned, many of those wounded. They left behind comrades, over 900 dead, and all the Canadian-attacking force's equipment and vehicles.

A dozen Canadian motorcyclists were directly involved in the raid. The bikes were fitted with four-foot snorkels to prevent sea water from drowning the engine, while the magnetos were covered in Plasticine for waterproofing; both were only partially successful modifications.

The Canadian DRs were assigned the task of charging around the Dieppe area on their Nortons, blowing up railway tracks, power and telephone lines and generally causing as much havoc as possible. Each Norton was packed with sixty pounds of anti-tank explosives and each DR carried another sixty pounds on his back.

George Meadows made it seventy feet up the beach before he and his bike were hit. Although he doesn't remember being picked up, he was one of the fortunate injured to make it back to England. Clarence Hardwick was the only DR on his landing craft. "We arrived at daylight; the Infantry had already landed when we hit the shore. The whole bridge of our landing craft was blown off, killing the captain of the craft and our major. It was plain hell once the ramp was dropped; the shells hit us, blowing my bike to pieces. Lucky we guys were behind the tanks. No one got very far, the tanks getting bogged down on the stony beach, losing their tracks.

"Of the twelve DRs and two jeeps loaded with explosives, none got off the beach. After about eight hours of action, we were told to get out the best way we could. I was one of the lucky ones, able to get to one of the boats able to leave. I only got minor shrapnel injuries."

The many others unable to retreat either died where they fell or faced almost three years of harsh Nazi imprisonment. There were more Canadians taken prisoner that day than during the entire northwestern European campaign of 1944-1945.

Dozens more DRs participated in the return of the troops, escorting "motor-coaches and lorries"[30] loaded with survivors to camps and casualty clearing stations. Others delivered lists of the survivors' names to CMHQ.

## SGT JIM CONWAY

RCCS

In 1939, Jim Conway enlisted with the RCCS as a DR in No. 1 DR Section. No. 1 Section was unique.

"Prior to the war, I was a member of a motorcycle club. We all joined the Militia (RCCS) for the fun and the cheap beer. When war was declared, fifteen of us enlisted as a group, with hardly a clue as to what we were getting into. This formed the nucleus of the section.

"We were sent to Kingston around October where we were brought up to strength with other recruits, mostly from Montreal. We arrived in England in January 1940, as a unit, known as 1st Canadian Details, RCCS, attached to the 1st Canadian Division in Aldershot. We got our bikes in March.

"Most of the bikes were Norton 500 cc side-valves. They weren't fast but they were reliable and a good bike for off-road use. There was one BSA 500 in the lot and I grabbed it."

The section operated in the area from London to Brighton, and from Salisbury to Dover, on regular scheduled runs. "In spite of the poor weather and narrow roads, we got to love the country and thought we had the best job in the army."

One privilege they enjoyed was the use of their bikes when off duty. This helped immeasurably in getting to know a strange land that, since Dunkirk, was without signposts. The signs had been removed to confuse the enemy in the event of invasion, "but it sure as hell confused a lot of our people. By using our bikes on unofficial training to explore the surrounding country, the knowledge we gained more than paid for the gas we used. It was also a neat way to pick up girls."

DRs were very possessive about their bikes. They resented anyone who borrowed them, especially those who did not know how to ride or look after them. "Our fitter [mechanic], who was also my brother [Joe Conway], took exception to Cement Head [the CSM] who regularly ordered that a bike be made available for him. He was a terrible rider with an irritating habit of starting the bike on its stand, kicking it into gear, then riding away, puttering around without changing gears. Played hell with the chains and valves.

**Above: The soggy roads of sunny Italy made travel by motorcycle extremely difficult.**

"One day, after being told to get a bike ready again, Joe decided to train him. He parked the bike about ten feet in front of a closed garage door and tightened the steering damper down as far as possible. Sure enough, Cement Head got on the bike, started it, put it in gear, pushed it off the stand, and accelerated right into the door! He wasn't hurt too badly, but he never requested the use of a bike again."

In the summer of 1940, Conway was promoted to sergeant. First Canadian Details was transferred to the Epsom area, working out of Corps HQ. "We had several scheduled runs each day plus three riders on duty shift for special runs. This is when we began to earn our pay!"

A war leaves vivid memories for those involved, and not always resulting from the conflict. A war takes young men to foreign lands full of the unfamiliar.

"A run I will always remember was one out to Salisbury Plain. The 5th Armoured Division was located there in the mud. It was late afternoon but quite an easy trip of about forty to fifty miles. I arrived about 6 p.m. It was after dark when I picked up the despatches but the moon was up and there was no traffic.

"On the way out, I noticed Stonehenge over to the left and made a mental note to ride out sometime to see them. Coming back, past Stonehenge rising on the right in the moonlight, is an experience I will never forget. It looked so foreboding that I could actually feel my skin crawl. It was a straight road across the moor and I had that old Norton full out until I was out of sight of those stones. Maybe some of my ancestors had worked for the Druids. I never did go back."

First Canadian Details had acquired the reputation of being rebels. As part of the effort to straighten out this motley crew, the CSM had them moved to the rear of the sergeants' quarters. No doubt the proximity to the voice of discipline and reason seemed like a good idea at the time. However, between the sergeants' and the DRs' quarters lay a storeroom full of brass band equipment.

"After a session in the wet canteen, the whole DR section decided to have a parade and broke into the storage room. They took the trumpets and drums and marched down the main street past the NAAFI [Navy, Army, Air Force Institute]. The Limeys and the girls at the canteen couldn't believe it. Leading the parade was a chap named Pelley. All he was wearing were rubber boots, a jockstrap, and a tin helmet, while twirling a plumber's plunger for a baton!

"Fortunately the CO had a sense of humour and nearly died laughing. He refused to allow Cement Head to prefer charges.

"One of the worst assignments we had was in 1942. We were awakened by a lot of aircraft of all sorts and couldn't figure out what was happening. Then I got a call from HQ to take half my section and report to the Harbour Master at Portsmouth. We all thought that we were going across the channel. We arrived in the middle of the worst bombing raid I have experienced."

It was the aftermath of Dieppe. The decks of incoming ships were crowded with Canadian soldiers, many of them wounded. Conway and his crew worked all night and well into the next day delivering lists of the names and condition of the survivors to CMHQ in London. The reality of war had docked at Portsmouth.

In the summer of 1943, 1st Canadian Details shipped out of Clyde, Scotland, rumoured to be headed for Africa. "We were lucky. We pulled an American Liberty ship with American rations. We were fed twice a day at stand-up tables, but you could eat all you wanted. Things like white bread and other luxuries were certainly appreciated."

Weather on the open sea was beautiful, and the DRs tanned amid submarine alerts.

"It was interesting watching the destroyers racing around like powerboats dropping depth charges. Don't know if they got anything but they sure blew the bottom out of the Mediterranean!"

Sometime after midnight, the night of 4-5 July, the convoy was attacked by enemy dive bombers. "That is the worst possible feeling, being below the decks on a ship during an air attack. I'll take a slit trench anytime." Two ships, the *St. Essyly* and the *City of Venice*, went down, taking almost all of Divisional HQ's vehicles and signal equipment with them.

Conway landed in Sicily at night, got some sleep in a staging camp, and woke to sunshine at the foot of Mt. Etna. From there, he and his fellow DRs hitched a ride with transport to HQ at Taormina to pick up their equipment: a couple of abused bikes and a water truck, leftovers from the British campaign in Africa. Because the water truck was the only thing that worked with any regularity, it became the principal vehicle for DR duty. "We were never short of water in our section!"

In early January of 1944, 1st Canadian Details crossed the Straits of Messina to Italy, and by March, now boasting a full complement of vehicles, joined up with the rest of 1st Canadian Corps eight miles south of Ortona in a town called Rocca San Giovanni.

Italy was drenched daily by heavy rains. The front bogged down. Dirt roads turned into swamps as the heavy clay of the area transformed into mud more than a foot deep. It clogged under motorcycle fenders and locked the wheels solid. The bikes were near useless on anything except paved roads, so the DRs began using jeeps.

"When the good weather finally arrived, everything came back to normal and we could use all of our vehicles. Then in May, we moved back across Italy for the attack on the Hitler Line through Cassino. Although we travelled through the mountains at night in convoy, it was easy because the Traffic Control and Military Police looked after the whole operation." The credit for the success and speed of these large-scale transfers of Canadian troops across the difficult terrain of Italy goes in large part to the No. 1 Provost Company, whose responsibility it was to keep traffic moving.

"After the breakthrough of the Hitler Line, the Canadians were pulled aside to let the Americans take Rome. We were camped in the Liri Valley which was a beautiful area. Our runs were quite easy and we ran from Naples to Rome. For a change, we had lots of time on our hands. The only sad part was that it was here that I received word that my youngest brother had been killed in a training accident in England.

"About this time, I had a run-in with a stupid officer, and to protect his health, they transferred me to the artillery as signal sergeant. After running a DR section for all those years, it was like going on vacation."

Of the original fifteen members of the motorcycle club who had enlisted together, fourteen survived to return to Canada after more than five years of overseas duty.

**Even flooded roads could not prevent the message from getting through. This DR had aspirations of arriving dry by keeping his feet up high.**

Canadian riders operated their bikes in nearly all parts of the world Canadian soldiers served during this global conflict—Canada, Newfoundland, USA, England, Italy, central and northwest Europe, Iceland, West Indies, Hong Kong, Malta, North Africa and India. About the only place Canadian soldiers went where no record of riders exists was the 1943 Allied invasion of the Aleutian Islands off the coast of Alaska.

On 10 July 1943 a combined Allied force invaded Sicily, and by 3 September the troops were on the mainland of Italy. On 6 June 1944, better known as D-Day, the largest Allied force to date landed in Normandy.

It was dusk when the transport ship carrying George Cuthill of the 2nd Security Section, Canadian Intelligence Corps, 2nd Division, arrived off the coast of Gold Beach, Normandy. "The rumour was that the enemy had mini-subs lurking in the area and that no one would land until daybreak. We already knew from the grapevine about the heavy casualties that 3rd Division had suffered, especially the number that had been lost between ship and shore, so we were quite anxious to get our feet on land again.

"After breakfast, we went up on deck and in due course, my Norton was lowered into the landing barge. I went over the side and down the scramble net to join it. It started easily and I sat there warming it up to be sure everything was okay. One of the sailors asked if I was scared, a foolish question, for anyone who said 'no' was lying. He tried to be helpful by telling me that when we landed, we would be in about ten feet of water, but not to worry, they would do their best to get me out. 'We don't lose many,' he said."

As Cuthill couldn't swim and was burdened down with a full pack, ammunition, and Sten gun, the sailor's words proved to be of little comfort. The barge started in for shore. "As soon as the ramp went down, I gunned the Norton, let out the clutch, and left the barge like a bullet, hoping to get as far as possible."

What Cuthill couldn't see from his position down in the barge was that the tide was going out, leaving the front of the ramp high and dry on the beach. "I was half a mile into France before I could stop! When I circled back, my navy friend was holding his sides in laughter. I had made his day."

Weather was to play an important role on both European fronts. The thaws and freezes of spring left a good part of Europe knee-deep in mud. Yet even if the armour couldn't get through, the messages did. When the flooded roads of Holland disappeared under the weight of the tanks, DRs resorted to rowboats to get by stalled traffic. "One thing that had been learned well already was the priceless value of good and timely information."[31]

In the heat of southern Italy, with troops exhausted from the rapid advance and transport scarce, motorcyclists broke the rules and gave soldiers a lift.

The following excerpts from the *RCMP Quarterly* give graphic testimony of the trials of being a provost in Italy.[32]

**The Cameron Highlanders of Ottawa in Iceland, 1940.**

On Sicily:

> It was on this island in the Mediterranean that our men first experienced traffic work under mortar and shell fire. A road junction is a place to be avoided, and drivers rush their vehicles by at top speed. Provost pointsmen, however, must remain, for it is essential that no tie-ups or jams occur and provide more profitable targets. . . . When enemy fire or weight of traffic destroys a bridge or road—and they frequently did—it is up to the provost to find a way around, or hold up traffic until the damage has been repaired. . . . The company was fortunate in Sicily. It suffered only one or two battle casualties. . . . Fatigue rising from long hours of duty caused a number of motorcycle accidents. . . it had its share of close shaves too, and some vehicles were damaged by enemy fire.

Regarding the east coast of Italy's mainland:

> Clearing the roads of civilian traffic became an irksome task. . . . Tanks and guns churned up mud on detours and at times rendered them impassable. For the first time in Italy, pointsmen were stationed at the forward extremity of vehicle movement to prevent drivers from running blindly into danger. . . . Pointsmen, patrolmen and section HQ are frequently under shell fire. . . . Casualties were a usual and commonplace thing on the Ortona front, but in our small close-knit company the loss of four killed and two wounded in one day was serious. . . .

The approach to Rome:

> Over the dirt tracks hung a constant dust cloud so thick that vehicle lights

**RCE sappers assist a DR up a steep, newly constructed road in Sicily, 6 September 1943.**

**A Coulombe of the Calgary Regiment attempts to catch up on some lost sleep. The cushion wrapped around the rear of the gas tank made riding upon the tank more comfortable. During advances, DRs carried all their belongings with them, as evidenced on this heavily laden Norton.**

frequently were necessary even though the sun shone brightly overhead. Our pointsmen, especially, suffered from the dust; they had to stand on their corners and take it and became so coated with grime that they were usually and quite literally unrecognizable. A few rain showers, short and sharp, turned the dust to mud for spells of an hour or so, bringing welcome relief to the pointsmen, but these added to the difficulties of our motorcyclists as they chugged up and down the far-reaching columns.

The return to Italy's Adriatic coast:

Occasional trouble arose with Polish Corps drivers who persisted in going the wrong way on one-way routes. . . .

**Thick mud slows this rider's advance through Italy, October 1943.**

Through the Falaise Gap in France, even with the enemy in retreat, the troops could advance only if transport was able to keep pace, which transport could do only if guided by the DRs. Troops were under daily bombings, occasionally even by Allied planes. And, of a more serious nature to some, European brothels were placed out of bounds.

In North Africa, the riders faced blinding sandstorms with their inadequate goggles. Often, they physically forced their bikes through thick, shifting sands.

## SGT RED BULLMAN

RCAF

"When you're on a bike, and you're out in North Africa halfway from Cairo and Tunisia or Tripoli or something like that, and something happens, you don't say, 'I'll send it back over to Ottawa.' You start right there. Fixing it."

Bullman enlisted in the RCAF in May 1939 as a mechanic, four months before Canada gave official notice of its intentions to go to war. "I knew the war was going to go anyway.

"Originally, when I went over, I was in 110 Squadron, RCAF." This was the first squadron Canada sent over to England, arriving at Odiham 25 February 1940. By March 1941 it had been renamed the 400 as part of a reorganization of RCAF squadron numbers to conform with those assigned to their British counterparts.

"There was no training for bikes in the air force. For example, we needed a despatch rider at Odiham in England. They said, 'Have you got somebody that can despatch ride?' I said 'Yeah, Hank—that's the boy right there. Hank, you want to ride a bike?' 'Yeah sure.' 'You're now a despatch rider. So here's a hat, you're going to need that, and a leather jacket.' He rode a bike for about two years.

"For a while in England, I had my own bike, a civilian Triumph I bought for five pounds, sidecar and everything. We took the sidecar off and camouflaged it, and put a military sticker on it so it looked like a despatch bike. You didn't need a license. I rode that all over the place using 100 octane.

"Now a Limey wouldn't do that. You know that.

"Sometimes, when in England, I'd have to go and get parts. And I'd want it now, like yesterday. So I would just take a bike and go up to Carlisle, near Scotland, or something like that, pick it up and come back. It was the fastest way to get there.

"I was in England for twenty-one months, and then they formed 417 [a new squadron which Bullman became part of]. They sent us all up to Thames, Scotland, and got us in shape for what we would be doing, with pith helmets and all that crap, then back over to Glasgow and on ship."

The ship was the *Aoragi*, which sailed south 13 April 1942 in a convoy to Durban, South Africa, final destination Egypt. This circuitous route around the southern tip of the African continent was chosen to avoid the Mediterranean where the enemy enjoyed overwhelming submarine and aircraft superiority. Yet even with this precaution, two ships were lost en route.

**Above: A DR of the RCAF dons high-gauntlet gloves in preparation for his next ride.**

"I'm standing right there. I watch one ship going boom over there, that was only about a hundred yards that direction on starboard side, and in another twenty minutes, boom, one right behind us. You didn't know if somebody was fixing in on you or not. Both went down in half an hour each. That was it.

"If it was your ship that got hit, lots of luck. You'd better get yourself a big plank and start swimming. A convoy can't stop. If they do, then somebody else can shoot on that. You don't know who's doing it, you see."

The *Aoragi* reached Durban 18 May. Seven days later, the equipment and troops of the 417 were loaded onto the *Mauretania*. This time, their ship sailed alone without the protection of a convoy, reaching Port Tewfik, Egypt, 4 June. From there they marched to Kasfareet. Under daily air attack by the enemy, Bullman's outfit moved on to Deversoir at the head of Bitter Lakes to act as the servicing squadron for No. 12 Mitchell Bombers, Group USAAF.

"That's the hottest goddamn place in the world! We had a new aerodrome there near Bitter Lakes along the canal. Now when the temperature gets up to about 140, the asphalt is just like soup. When the Americans were transporting their stuff in there, they'd come in with a B25, loaded. Really loaded. And you could see the damn thing starting to slow down, and as it slows down, you just see it sink. Clean right over the axles into the asphalt!

"And the sand, from there on. I can taste it yet, the goddamn sand!" It clung tenaciously to food, clothing and skin, yet refused to hold a tent peg in place.

In September, the 417 inherited the worn-out Hurricane fighter planes and equipment from the Fighting French Alsace Squadron. Not long after, the Hurricanes were replaced with Spitfires.

"You never know where you're going, they just tell you. Geez, on one trip I had there I went all the way from Suez to Tripoli. That's over seventeen hundred miles. And I did that with my convoy."

It was long days of frustrating desert travel escorting a lethargic, metallic snake of armoured machinery through the heat and sandstorms. "I ran that convoy. I did all the transport work for over fifty vehicles. That was when the war was moving west. We had to keep everything going with it for our Spits (Spitfires). All the goddamn stuff and the long-range tanks and that. So you see, when you're on those narrow roads, and something breaks down, what are you going to do? Sit there? To hell with that!

"I had a great big diesel truck and a trailer on the back. That is what I slept in at night. I ran a motorcycle all day. It took us three weeks to get there, and I'll bet you I put four thousand miles on the bike! Back and forth along the convoy. That's my equipment—that's all my vehicles. I had another guy by the name of Rainville from Montreal, and Rainville and I did all our policing and everything else.

"Christ, in North Africa, I rode a bike practically all the time. I had one three-ton truck, four-wheel drive, with all the hoops and all that crap off it, so that you could go. And it was tuned up and sitting there all the time. And I had one bike, a BSA V-twin, sitting there.

"If I wanted to go to Cairo, or wherever I had to go, many times it's a hell of a lot faster to go by bike. Want to go some place? I'm going on a bike.

"When we first got there, we had tents. It was one of those situations where, you put up a tent, you get her all nailed down, and you're all set. Christ, tomorrow, in the morning you take it down. In the afternoon—no we're not going to move today.

"The enemy was still twenty-two miles from Cairo, sitting there. We're on one side, and they're on the other. They didn't move; neither had us.

Faster than a speeding mule, Canadian DRs Paul Riopel, Bill Stemmler and F. A. Davies make good time on a rare paved road in North Africa.

"So one day I was all set to do this again, and there was the tent and pickets and all the goddamn crap. An AC2 Limey walked by and I said, 'You want a tent? Here, take the goddamn thing! I don't want to ever see it or you!'

"From there on I slept in the truck. Right in the back. You take a rope twice across the rack, and tie on the mosquito net, get in, and you're all set. No mosquitos, nice clean, no bugs.

"Three of us lived in the back of that truck. We were the three bike riders.

"We got up near a couple of hundred miles before you get to Tripoli, and my workshop was a way behind. We were supposed to be stopping at an area we had for lunch. The cookhouse was going to be there for twelve noon.

"But—I can't think of his name—a guy from Winnipeg, got a flat on his bike, so the workshop truck stopped to repair the flat. I didn't see my workshop truck, so I went back and the boys were repairing the bike in the back of the truck.

"The convoy needed the bike, so when we finished it up, the rider said, 'I'll go ahead.' We were probably twenty to twenty-five miles behind now.

"I rode back but the rider wasn't there. I had ridden right past him. He was doing about seventy, and some bastard had pulled up a piece of telephone line. He got caught right in the neck. Now it didn't tear his head off, fortunately, because the wire snapped. But oh, you should have seen his neck. Holy christ!

"It flipped him off the bike, but it didn't knock him out. They were hoping to get his gun and the bike. But he was standing there when my work truck came up. We put him and the bike in the back and took him to an ambulance. His next stop was Canada.

"Eventually, I picked up an Italian great big diesel Alfa Romeo truck. We got double tarps to put on that with hoops over the back, and we acquired a piano. I forget where the hell that came from. We toted that thing, I'd don't know where the hell it eventually went."

Throughout the Egyptian campaign, Bullman was fortunate to be able to pursue his passion for music. His squadron had a band; Danny Marples on guitar and base, Johnny Koplitz, the trumpet-playing leader, two others whose names have been lost in time, and Bullman on accordion. These were serious musicians who developed a well-earned reputation, both on- and offstage. Of their musical talents, their CO had this to say: "We have the finest five-piece swing band in the desert, led by P/O Johnny Koplitz of

Hoboken, former American band leader, and greatly in demand by army and air force units far and near. Lacking movies and concert parties, this band filled in many a dull evening."

Bullman tells of one such dull evening. "When we got to Tripoli, we got in a little bit of a tiny hassle. One of our guitar players, he got stonked, and he made a hell of a lot of noise. We tried to cover him, so the next day we were going to be on charge. So we saw the boss, the local CO, and told him a little lie that we had a chance to transport with the Americans.

"They were so goddamn happy to hear of us getting out of there, they gave us permission. Well Jesus, you can't do that, but he transferred us from Canadians to Americans! That was the paper we had for six of us!" The war diary for the 417 Squadron notes only that on 27 May 1943 an "adjutant and four senior NCOs granted leave and air transportation to Alex."

"We hitchhiked over to the airport, and when the Americans saw us, they thought we were Limeys. But as soon as they saw us wearing Canada, they said, 'Oh shit, where do you want to go?' 'Cairo'. 'Sit down.'

"They took us out fishing in the afternoon on the Mediterranean and fed us and everything, and the next morning, put us on a DC3 to Cairo. In fact, I flew the goddamn DC3!

"The captain was going to India, and he was tired, so he said, 'I want to sleep, you fly.' I said I never flew that one. 'Well you're going to learn right now, take the wheel.' So I flew the damn thing all the way to Cairo. I was happy to get out of there, boy!

"We had about a week off sitting around, then the ship started and we got all the way to Tunisia, then Algiers, and to England.

"I didn't have much in the way of kit when I got that finished, an Irving jacket and one pair of slacks.

"I was sitting on my butt for another couple of weeks before they decided where I was going to go next. It was two weeks of rest camp. But every morning at nine o'clock, you had to be on the parade square. It didn't matter what the hell you wore. You could wear nothing because it was all men, they didn't give a shit! But you had to be there. Because there was going to be a list, and you'd hear names.

"One morning, I get called. Next, I get on a ship. From there, I came back to Canada.

"I arrived back in December 1943 in time for Christmas. I ended up in Uplands running the transport. I took over Works and Breaks too—bulldozers and everything.

"About in May or June of '44, I bought another bike, a Norton single. That was my own.

"After the war was over, Christ, they wanted to parade! Every morning! So I started balking. I don't like that kind of business. So they kept yapping and I kept yapping.

"I said I can't do two things or three things at the same time. Well you're going to have to. Well, I said you're not going to get any transport. No, we have to have more on this and that and the other thing. So we argued.

"Then, I went back over to my office, pulled out the typewriter and some paper, and wrote myself a resignation—three copies—and I was out."

Bullman settled in North Bay, Ontario, and continued to ride motorcycles until his death in 1988.

Snipers were everywhere and the motorcyclist was an easy target.

> Holland, April 16, 1945: Capt E. V. Ardagh left at 0900 hrs to recce routes and the area for a HQ at Peeler. With him went the Provost Sgt, Sgt Carpick, on a motorcycle. At Otterlo, they encountered small arms fire and motar fire from enemy troops. After a short battle, the recce party withdrew bringing with them four prisoners but minus one motorcycle.

Because DRs were often unable to hear gunfire over the roar of their motorcycles' engine, they became easy targets for enemy troops, although, as Russ Ridler of 12 Platoon, C Company, Toronto Scottish Regiment explains, sometimes there were other means by which a rider could detect he was under fire.

"We were in and around the town of Ifs, holding our positions against a Panzer Division while the American forces were cutting across from the north. I was riding back from an O Group when a sniper put a shot in my gas tank, close to my knees. I hesitate to tell you what colour I turned.

"After regaining my composure, I plugged the hole with a twig wrapped in a four-by-two-inch bandage. Naturally, my exploits of being in combat were perhaps exaggerated upon my return to Company HQ."

The enemy set traps specifically aimed at bagging a DR—telephone lines strung across roads at neck height, oil poured over paved corners, abandoned motorcycles booby-trapped, even horse manure was strategically placed in hopes of catching an inattentive DR off guard.

With no signs and few points of reference still standing, there was always the danger of getting lost or simply riding into enemy territory:

> Nov 23, 1944: 1420 hrs an excited telephone call from 5 CAB (Canadian Armoured Brigade). A DR from that HQ had been sent to the Westminster Regt and had started out via Highway 16, the main north-south road in Italy running from Canadian lines into the enemy's. The DR was last seen riding unconcernedly up the road. Nothing further was heard from him. It was found later he was carrying invitations to the dance held by 5 CAB in Cervia.

## SGT NORM BRAULT

### Westminster Regiment, 5th Canadian Armoured Division

A wet, battlefield-black night swallowed Italy, saturating the air and earth, converting dirt to mud. Brault lay in a hole dug for him by his comrades, his right leg swollen to near twice its normal size, throbbing, his face cut and bleeding. A scrap of corrugated metal covered the hole, shielding him from the rain.

A barrage of 5.5-inch artillery guns began to fire, one after another after another, stonking an enemy only a short distance to the north. And each time the artillery of the 5th Canadian Armoured Division fired, Italy shook, lifting Brault's body for an instant, then letting it fall hard to the ground. Incessantly, the guns pounded enemy positions and the rain pounded on the metal roof and the pain pounded in his right leg. Perhaps Brault now questioned why he had refused to leave for the sanctuary of a hospital.

Originally, Brault had not thought of himself as a person burdened with a strong sense of duty. He had joined the army in 1940 at the age of nineteen and became a DR so that he could continue to play his double-B-flat tuba, a task he though preferable to carrying a rifle. The Westminster Regiment Band was an unofficial unit, and therefore, all the members had to have real military jobs. Brault liked the idea of being a DR ("no marching"). Now, he wasn't so sure he had made the right decision.

Perhaps it was the gnawing pain, or the severity of that dark pit that engulfed him, or the terror of the guns blasting the night all around him. Or maybe it was simply that he was now so totally alone. Whatever the reasons, Brault began to cry.

"In early November 1943 we left Liverpool for Italy. Like any troopship, we were packed in like sardines, restless from boredom, and the food was bad. I remember going through the Strait of Gibraltar just barely seeing the rock at night. On the right, Tangiers, North Africa, being neutral, was all lit up. This was the first time we had seen a city lit up. Quite a feeling."

On 6 November the hospital supply ship in the convoy was sunk, so Brault's ship put into Algiers where the troops disembarked, allowing the ship to return to England for medical supplies. The troops meanwhile carried on by train ("previously occupied by sheep") to Philippeville, and then by boat to Naples.

"Naples was very depressing with all the sunken ships in the harbour. We were

**Above: Norm Brault (right) with two fellow DRs.**

**DR J. K. Armstrong, RCCS, parks his Triumph to accept a message from Sgt R. H. Easby at 5th Canadian Armoured Division HQ, Catelnouvo, Italy, 17 March 1944.**

trucked over to a village called Afragola, bedded down in tents on the frozen ground, with Mount Vesuvius puffing up flames in the background."

From here, they were transferred to Matera, a town built into the caves about forty kilometres north of the Gulf of Taranto. Brault spent his first Italian Christmas there, which also coincided with his first contact with *vino rosso*—"Disastrous!

"Just previous to this, we received our so-called new equipment, all leftovers from the African do."

At the time, few ships were available for such large undertakings as the 5th Armoured Division's transfer to Italy, so in order to get the troops there, they were sent on without equipment. It was agreed that the Canadians would inherit the guns and transports of British formations returning to England. When the British in Italy got wind of this, they quickly swapped their bad equipment for the good of those troops returning, which left the Canadians in possession of a lot of junk. A fair percentage of the equipment they were to take to the front broke down before it even got to Matera. Brault was issued an old, mildly dilapidated, tan-painted BSA M20 with a sand filter over the carburetor.

During the month spent in training at Matera, some new equipment began to arrive, and the day the Division left for the front, Brault, along with three other DRs, was issued a brand new Triumph.

As the Division approached their destination, the Sangro River, they could see the flash of the guns over the ridge, each followed by a boom—gunfire and explosion, gunfire and explosion—linked together like the improvised notes of a scat singer performing in hell. All the training, in Canada, in England, and in southern Italy, was about to be tested. Mistakes would no longer be excused. To Brault, it was "scary and exciting and cold."

**Many rivers had to be crossed en route to the 5th Canadian Armoured Division's destination of Sangro River. Here, sapper J. Hancheroff, 3rd Field Company, RCE, and Gnr L. McDermott, 54th LAA help DR W. White (peaked cap), 54th LAA, wrestle his Norton across the Biferno River.**

The Division moved into a group of farmhouses.

Both the enemy and the Allies held their lines, each side trying to find and nibble at their opponent's weaknesses with endless patrols. Snipers, mines, piano wire strung across roads, radio silence—it ate at the nerves of young soldiers. And for the first time, the Westminster Regiment suffered casualties—friends killed and wounded.

At night, the valleys fell silent and black. Each side knew the patrols were out there, unseen, crawling on their bellies through the brush and dirt until, *gun fire!*, patrol finds patrol.

"Each company had its own village or farmhouse. It was a horrible situation—cold, mud, snow, and huge vats of *vino rosso.* I remember very well one of the officers using his tommy gun to blast some of the barrels, letting the wine run down the streets. What a waste!"

At times, the terrain was so rough, all DR work had to be carried out on foot as any machine less than a tank simply floundered in the hills. But whenever possible, Brault used the bike. "We always knocked out the baffle plates in the mufflers. This made more noise, giving us the feeling of more power."

While the benefits of these modifications were mostly theoretical, there was one definite advantage resulting from the increased noise levels. Unfortunately, that advantage lay with the enemy. They could hear the movements of the DRs much better.

Brault left the Signals HQ with a despatch for B Company. Daylight was fading fast, consumed by the chill of a winter's night. He rode into dusk, around the carcass of a fallen white cow, and aimed up a ridge. The bike bogged down in a snowbank. Brault dismounted, and with full muscle and full throttle, forced the machine forward. The clear, still air of the mountains reverberated with the wail of a howling unmuzzled exhaust. Brault made his destination just as the mortars descended.

"I delivered the despatch, but it was pretty wild for a few minutes. My BSA [Brault doesn't mention what became of his Triumph!] was sort of a dog, and when I finally hauled myself out of the farmhouse, I was hoping it would be all blasted to hell, but no, there it was, all covered with mud and snow! I kicked it over and got the hell out of there fast."

The return trip was made in complete darkness as the use of lights was not permitted. Brault rode fast, driven by the fear of deadly enemy patrols. Nighttime was prime time for snipers and sabotage. He roared down the ridge that had stopped him on the way to the front, around blind curves in pitch black, into valleys thick with apprehension, and smack into the carcass of a white cow. Brault and the bike went down.

At times like this a DR can pay dearly for his cherished independence. He rides alone, and he falls alone. Fortunately, dead cows tend to be more forgiving to crash into than rocks or tanks. Brault escaped injury and made it back to HQ.

During April and early May of 1944, 1st Canadian Corps, which included the 1st Infantry Division and Brault's 5th Armoured Division, were secretly transferred to the Cassino front to help with the Allied push to Rome. Fighting along this front became so severe that at one point, a two-hour truce was declared so the dead and wounded could be removed from the battlefield below Montecassino.

The area was a nightmare for travel—narrow gravel roads that twisted through the mountains along countless switchbacks and sheer drop-offs. To aid night travel, white tape was strung out along the edges of the highest cliffs, but it was still a treacherous adventure illuminated only by the flash of the guns.

The route was under constant observation of the enemy, so riders were instructed to shut off their engines on the descent and coast. Guns blasted in the distance, sending echoes rolling through the valleys, crashing against mountain walls like waves against a rocky shoreline. Coasting in the dark among the flickering ghosts of shell fire, the rider listened, straining to *hear* the hidden curve and darkened cliff. Gravel talks through the tires of a bike. What was that? Probably just the creak and groan of an abused and worn motorcycle. Or was it the death crawl of a sniper?

The Canadians eased along the front to the point where they could see the remains of Cassino and the monastery. The shelling was constant, as were the casualties, while a rough and battered terrain once again prevented the use of vehicles. "We used real mean North African mules [about 2,000] to bring up ammunition and rations with African mule skinners."

The 1st Canadian Corps was then called back down the mountain to prepare for the big push against the Senger and Gustav lines. The objective of the 5th Armoured Division was the Senger Line, an imposing series of fortified positions running between Piedmonte, Aquino, and Pontecorvo (originally, the enemy referred to this line as the Hitler Line; the name swap occurred when the line became threatened by the Allies). After a few days of lectures and weapon and machinery cleaning, the Canadians moved into position.

Brault and his company spent the night in a sheltered, quiet grove of trees as the artillery moved in behind them. At dawn, 230 guns opened fire on the enemy over a 2,400-yard-wide area ("It just about lifted us right off the ground!"), and the troops were soon charging into battle.

**Italy, summer of 1943.**

The weather was stunning—warm, full sunshine, and clear. Queen Victoria's birthday, 24 May 1944. The Senger Line had been breached, and units of the 5th Armoured Division had already crossed the Melfa River.

"Coming into the Liri valley, the noise was tremendous—the shell fire and mortars. I felt so naked, with a gas tank between my legs and a steel helmet and everyone in the ditch and others with their hatches down."

As Brault rode toward the Melfa, he kept encountering the wounded, from both sides, and the prisoners. The Benedictine crossroads was a brawl of ear-splitting sounds, burning tanks, bodies and heavy shelling. "Close-growing scrub restricted visibility and movement, and the Westminsters were hard put to it to follow the armour across irrigation ditches and over ground covered with stumps and fallen trees."[33]

"I kept saying to myself, what a beautiful day and yet all this horror."

Brault was given a despatch to deliver to Major Mahony (who won a Victoria Cross in this action). The Major's company had established a small beachhead on the other side of the Melfa. From the crossroads, it was about a quarter mile to the river. The trip had to be made on foot.

About halfway to the river, three Irish Regiment of Canada soldiers had taken refuge behind a rock. One was wounded and the other two called out to Brault to give them a hand. Brault kept running.

"I wanted to help but the first priority was the despatch. You should have heard what they called me. I never to this day forgot that. I don't think I was yellow, having to cross that waist-high river in a fifteen-miles-per-hour current with everything landing all around."

Brault had to make the same run again, although without the taunts of his fellow soldiers this time. "We lost a great deal of good people that day, but accomplished our goal." Brault was hit in the lip, and now wears a moustache to cover the scar. "I'll tell you one thing, it sure smarted and knocked me down!

"There were so many acts of bravery. I am always upset with war historians in that the Canadians are very seldom mentioned."

The next day, the 5th Armoured Division continued its advance up the narrow Liri valley through congested traffic. The Westminster's War Diary notes that "bits and pieces of the Regt were all over the countryside, numerous vehicles being suspended over cliffs or jammed in sunken roads." Brault's company pulled into a grove of trees behind a knocked-out Sherman tank. Ahead lay Route 6, the road to Rome.

"We had just got our slit trenches dug when all hell broke loose. We could see the flash of the German gun just over the highway. Apparently, they didn't realize the tank ahead of us was already kaput. Anyway, it was landing all around us—armour-piercing, high explosive, which meant that it would pierce the armour and then explode inside the tank. This was quite a feeling when lying in a slit trench, the ammo digging into the ground and then exploding. It gave us a bit of a lift!"

The colonel sent the other HQ DR back to find a safer route but grew impatient waiting. He ordered Brault to remain and wait for his partner and departed with the company, leaving the two DRs to follow as best they could.

Brault lay in his slit trench. "What a lonely feeling, not a soul around except the enemy up ahead." His hosts continued to lob shells in his direction. Watching a tree fall down on top of him, he was convinced he had met his end, "but no damage done. After an eternity, the other DR, Reynan, returned and we cut across a big open field. That really excited the enemy, and they really laid it down!"

In the scramble to safety, a tree stump tore a footpeg off Brault's machine. Then his throttle snapped. "Reynan came back all hot and excited wanting me to keep up. I just threw the bike down, grabbed my saddlebags, climbed on behind him, and we got the hell out of there!

"It took us a few hours to find the colonel. There they were with the rest of the company parked in a nice little serene grove of trees. At least I finally got rid of the old gutless BSA. Our recovery unit never did find it."

On 31 May, 1st Corps was pulled back into reserve. On 4 June the Americans marched into Rome. The Canadians were then transferred back east to fight on the Gothic Line beside the Adriatic Sea.

"This was supposed to be a piece of cake." The enemy welcomed them with tank turrets cemented into pillboxes at strategic locations, minefields, and trenches. "They even put tanks into buildings and blew them down around them with just the guns showing. They were waiting for us."

Brault was issued an old Matchless—"What a dog!"—to replace his abandoned BSA. It proved to be a step backward.

"One day following the half-tracks up a steep hill cross-country under lots of mortars and shell fire, the machine just wouldn't pull the grade. There were lots of snipers in the area, so you didn't want to be stationary. I just laid it down, grabbed my saddle bags, and hitched a ride on a half-track. Lots of injuries that day."

This second abandonment netted Brault a reasonably new BSA, "a nice machine." On the 1 September the company stopped for the night at a small village called Tomba di Pesaro. "The shell fire and hot shrapnel set some straw stacks ablaze, making everyone feel quite naked." For Brault, it also brought back memories of the wiener roasts he and his friends had as kids back in Saskatchewan. The next morning, all memories were blown away as the village shook under an intense bombardment. There were more killed and wounded, but 1st Corps pushed on, driving the enemy back. Eventually, Brault's regiment was relieved by the Irish. It was while in the rest area that Brault was put out of action, and the enemy could not even take credit for it.

"We DRs found a nice little farmhouse to bed down in. The old Italian farmer gave us some *vechio vino bianco*. Lovely, but quite strong. Then came our rum issue. I felt like a thermometer, a nice rosy feeling."

This indulgence may have gone without mishap had Brault not been the Duty DR for the night, and had the adjutant not wanted a message taken back to Brigade HQ. Brault's perception of fear and the world now altered somewhat, he climbed aboard his BSA and roared off to fulfil this mission with enthusiasm. Farther back, the crossroads were under heavy fire, but Brault charged on through, throttle open, around the bend, and head on into a jeep full of Polish soldiers. He and his latest bike parted company.

It was this unsuccessful catapult over a jeep that bashed his leg, and his resultant refusal to head for a hospital that led him to a hole in the ground where, alone and in extreme pain, he cried as the rain fell and the guns roared.

The next morning, when an officer saw Brault's face and leg, no time was wasted in getting the sorry-looking soldier to the ADS (Advanced Dressing Station) and from there, back to Perugia and an old tobacco factory now serving as a hospital. Brault spent two months convalescing. "What a difference! White sheets, nurses, good food, everyone looking after you. It was so serene, for the first four days I couldn't sleep!"

This hardship eventually came to an end and Brault was shipped back to his regiment. He stepped off the truck right onto another tired and winded BSA and into action. And as comfy as those white sheets were, "It was nice to see my old comrades again."

It rained and snowed and was miserably cold, with a new river to cross every day. A welcome order came forth from 12th Brigade HQ: "Effective immediately winter underwear long, as issued, will be taken into wear." Ahead of the Westminsters lay the city of Ravenna, which the 5th Armoured Division captured 4 December, moving north then to encounter strong enemy resistance.

Despite the adverse conditions, during the first three weeks of December, 1st Corps DRs delivered more than twenty-eight thousand individual packets.[34] The fourth week, the Canadians pulled back to Ravenna for "a tremendous Christmas dinner—turkey, booze, the works!" Then it was back to the front, where both sides dug in for the winter. Patrols, shelling, casualties, and bad nerves. On 2 January 1945 the 5th Armoured Division took Conventelle. Ten days later, 1st Corps pulled back into reserve for the last time in Italy.

On 31 January they began the 315-mile journey across Italy once again, and on 22 February they set sail aboard the ship *Esperance Bay*, from Leghorn to Marseilles, the first contingent of 1st Corps troops to southern France. The transfer to Marseilles continued into March; the movements of the Corps were being carefully concealed from the enemy until their arrival in Holland.

Along the way, somewhere in Belgium, Brault finally got his hands on a Norton, just a few months before the war ended. This was a revelation in riding to him, and he made the best of its speed and reliability to stay out of trouble.

"There was this saying about the enemy never being worried about the Canadian

**Battered bridges and damaged power dams slowed the advance through Italy. The light weight and mobility inherent to the motorcycles of the Second World War allowed PPCLI DR Jerry Jobsey to pass over the remains of this dam near Colle d'Anchise, Italy, October 1943.**

soldier—just give them a bottle of whisky and a motorcycle and they would kill themselves!"

How lucky for Brault the author of that proverb neglected to include *vino* in the formula.

As the war neared its end, the four-wheel drive jeep began to take over much of the traditional DR work, all but replacing the motorcycle sidecar unit. Humber scout cars and even half-tracks were occasionally used too. Although the motorcycle, particularly the solo unit, was more manoeuvrable than other motorized vehicles, the motorcycle's capabilities were far more dependent upon operator skill, and the rider more vulnerable to sniper attacks. Yet, to the bewilderment of those in command, many riders resented the change, preferring to keep their bikes. No other vehicle could ever offer them so much freedom, and freedom was, after all, what the war was supposed to be about.

# APPROACHING A NEW CENTURY

Immediately following the Second World War, the role of Canada's military was not unlike the role it played after the First World War—serving as a unit of the Occupational Army in northwest Germany, with a few smaller administrative units stationed throughout Europe. The Canadian Army Occupation Force consisted of a revised 3rd Canadian Infantry Division, the bulk of the remaining troops having returned home to civilian life almost before the ink dried on the surrender documents. By June 1946 even this 3rd Division was back in Canada, and by December all Canadian HQs in Germany had been disbanded.

A year before the 3rd Division's return, Canada agreed to participate in an organization that would soon establish the nature of its military role in world affairs. On 26 June 1945 Canada, together with friends and foes of the past and present, signed the charter of United Nations (UN).

Canada's armed forces had been reduced to not much more than twenty thousand, consisting of a Mobile Striking Force (an airborne unit), coastal defence units and a small outfit of about twelve hundred whose specific task was to maintain and police the Alaska Highway and northern radio installations. Canada relied heavily upon its militia to supplement the

**Following the Second World War, Canadian DRs continued to provide escort duty, here for dignitaries of the Canadian Army Occupation Force in Aurich, Germany, 25 November 1945.**

permanent forces.

In addition to the UN, Canada joined the North Atlantic Treaty Organization (NATO) in 1949. An offshoot of this agreement was the understanding that the American, British and Canadian military would work toward standardization of military equipment. Another first was the exchange of military personnel with the US.

The advantages of co-ordinating the military efforts of close allies were soon realized when on 25 June 1950 North Korea invaded South Korea. Under the flag of the UN, troops were sent in to help defend South Korea. In August 1950 the Canadian Army Special Force was established as Canada's contribution to this effort. Much of the training took place with American troops at Fort Lewis, Washington. In February of the following year, Canadian defence spending was substantially increased, the number of Canadian armed forces personnel more than doubled, and much-needed new equipment purchased to replace the worn-out leftovers of an old war.

Motorcycles, although temporarily outpaced by other forms of transport from a technological standpoint, were not entirely forgotten in this buying splurge. The mobility of the two-wheeler had yet to be equalled by any other land-based vehicle, a statement which still holds true today.

Until this point, the principal motorcycles of the Canadian forces had continued to be the Norton 16H and Harley-Davidson WLC of Second World War vintage. During 1949, the US Airborne Service Test Division invited manufacturers to submit machines for a new category titled "Motorcycle, Solo, Extra Lightweight, T3," and in compliance with the standardization program, the results were forwarded to Canadian offices for consideration in its military plans.

Six manufacturers submitted machines for testing: the Whizzer Motor Company, Uni-Flo Engine Corporation, Jordan Motorcycle Corporation, Harley-Davidson Motor Company, the Indian Motorcycle Company and the Simplex Manufacturing Corporation. Each was to be tested in "speed trials, fordability, and performance in mud and sand, over rough terrain, and on roads."[35]

Although forewarned of the specifications and tests, most of the manufacturers came ill-prepared. The Uni-Flo Wheelmaster was merely a bicycle with a small engine bolted to the front wheel. It participated in the speed trials only and was understandably rated "impractical for adaptation to military use."

**DR Cecil Whidden of 25th Canadian Infantry Signal Squadron on exercise at Fort Lewis, Washington, 25 January 1951.**

Since the odd monocoque Jordan was the only such example in existence, its manufacturer did not permit it to enter any test in which it might be damaged, yet even with these restrictions, it was still judged to be "unstable to ride."

The little Whizzer struggled through all phases of the competition, but its small bicycle-type tires restricted its performance in sand and mud. There was also some question as to whether such a lightly constructed machine could withstand the rigors of military use.

The Servicycle Power Bike by Simplex (ten of which had already been used by Canadian DRs during the Second World War) would "not operate in all types of weather or terrain" and was also rejected.

Both the Indian Arrow, Model 149, and the Harley-Davidson Model 125 performed in all tests, although not exceptionally well, and the Indian was chosen for further tests to "determine the necessary military requirements of a vehicle of this type."

There is no evidence to suggest that Canada did anything but file the report.

Although some Canadian soldiers trained at Fort Lewis were taught motorcycle riding skills prior to their departure to Korea, only a few Nortons followed them over to get covered in Korean mud. However, during that period Harley-Davidson WLCs did see use on Canadian and German soil by the Provost Corps, particularly in traffic control, crowd control and escort duty when dignitaries went on parade, like Princess Elizabeth and the Duke of Edinburgh's 1951 visit to Canada for example.

When the Korea Armistice Agreement was signed in 1953, Canada chose to maintain its forces at the levels brought on by that conflict. At the time, it was an important decision that reflected Canada's commitment to world peace. Although the nation had participated in Korea as a combatant, until 1990 all military involvement with the UN was

Harley-Davidson Model 125.

Whizzer

Indian Arrow, Model 149

Uni-Flo Wheelmaster.

Jordan.

Servicycle Power Bike.

restricted to peacekeeping roles, Canadian forces acting primarily as observers to help maintain a UN-assisted truce. In fact, prior to joining the Allied Coalition to fight in the Persian Gulf War, Canada had taken part in more UN peacekeeping operations than any other nation.

There is no record that motorcycles were part of this commitment. The military definitely favoured the greater carrying capacity of jeeps, but motorcycles continued to be used for escort duty and in both Canadian and NATO military exercises, in Canada and abroad.

The RCCS continued to train DRs on motorcycles. The unit stationed at Wolsely Barracks in London, Ontario, used Nortons and Harleys until 1956, when it switched to the new bike of the Canadian army.

**L-Cpl George Trembley and L-Cpl Paul Harvey of the Royal 22nd Regiment force a Norton through the Korean landscape, 15 September 1951.**

**The Provosts on the white Harley-Davidsons obviously enjoyed a much smaller turning circle than their comrades in the dressed-up jeeps as the Company prepared to escort visiting royalty.**

**Cpl Frank "Tex" Davis on a Harley-Davidson escorts a convoy through Listowel, Ontario, to Camp Borden during 1954.**

In December of 1955, under the American-British-Canadian Armies Standardization Program, a new motorcycle was chosen to replace the Second World War remains of the Canadian and British armies, the Motor Cycle G. S. 500 cc Triumph Type TRW Mks 1 and 2 FV2000 Series (ABC-ARMY-STD-53). Although the US army signed the agreement with the clause "the United States Army interposes no objection to the promulgation of this standard," it chose to continue using Harleys in lieu of the offshore British Triumph. As a result of national pride (and perhaps economics), standardization would remain more a military ideal than a reality.

The TRW was designed with ease of control in mind, and made use of at least 80 percent civilian Triumph production motorcycle content. It was decidedly not a high-performance machine, and the lack of rear suspension and its excess weight restricted off-road capabilities. The TRW was in essence more in keeping with the Harleys of the US than the nimble British bikes of the Second World War, or especially the current civilian models. Its low-speed stability made it well suited for escort and parade duty, the common uses of the motorcycle as designated by the Canadian military.

This narrow view of how a motorcycle should participate in Canada's military was unfortunate, as opportunities to expand the motorcycle's role were missed. However, because of its inherent low-speed stability, the TRW did shine when it came to motorcycle rider display teams.

As primary users of motorcycles during the Second World War, the RCCS had continued its association with the machine despite the lack of interest or disenchantment of CMHQ. The RC Signals DR Display Team was originally formed under the guise of a recruitment tool—tour Canada, wow the guys, then get them to sign up. The team was

**1957 Triumph TRW**

formed in August 1952, training at the Canadian Signal Training Centre near Kingston, Ontario. Public appearances commenced in the spring of 1953 using antiquated Norton 16Hs and the very desirable Triumph Trophy. These were eventually replaced with TRWs.

The team was made up of thirty DRs who performed "spectacular tricks of acrobatic riding, interspersed with formation riding at high speeds with several jumps where riders hurtle over a high ramp through walls of brick and fire."[36] It was a show that never failed to amaze the public. In Quebec the team was billed as the Gear-shift and Transmission Company. For tricks that involved a rider standing upon another's shoulders, like the pyramid, those on the bottom would often put their gloves over their shoulders to prevent the sharp boot heels of the rider above from digging into the skin.

The team performed across Canada two years in a row entertaining the public at the

Calgary Stampede, Canadian National Exhibition, various county fairs and a few children's hospitals. The team was disbanded in 1956, a high-profile recruitment tool no longer deemed necessary.

The Provost Corps also had a motorcycle display team, which trained at Camp Borden in 1955, appearing publicly in the fall of that year. The Provost team used the heavy Harley-Davidson WLC, a bike not well suited to stunt riding, but it still managed to put on an exciting show full of tricks and precision riding.

After these display teams stopped actively functioning, not much was seen of the Canadian military motorcycle. Small numbers of TRWs were issued to militia units for use on escort duty during training convoys. With the arrival of two of the bikes at the University Avenue Armoury in Toronto, Allan Johnson, a young cadet with 5 Company, RCASC, recalls, "You could not hold sixty-five miles per hour for very long or you would get to ride home in the back of a truck since the head gasket would blow. Compared to the civilian OHV 500—well, there was no comparison."

A few TRWs continued to be used in a very limited role for despatch work in West Germany during the late 1950s and early 1960s and also during some exercises in Canada, but that was the extent of official use. At least until 1967.

As Canada's centennial year approached, it was decided to resurrect the display team idea as part of the military's contribution to the nation's birthday bash. Three teams, two in the Canadian Armed Forces Tattoo and one Canadian Armed Forces Motorcycle Display Team, began training together in May 1966 at the Vimy barracks, Kingston, Ontario.

**The RCCS Motorcycle Display Team performance heats up as a rider jumps through a ring of fire in Montreal, 9 July 1953.**

**The RCCS Motorcycle Display Team on 7th Avenue, Calgary, Alberta, 6 July 1954.**

The Tattoo Team was a precision riding outfit. The Display Team did precision rides too, and a host of stunts and tricks fashioned after the Display Team of the 1950s. Welcome help and tips were also offered by the Royal Marine Corps and Royal Corps of Signals motorcycle teams of the United Kingdom.

The teams began by using TRWs exclusively, even for the stunts, but soon found the bikes lacking when it came to jumps. Civilian model Triumph Tiger 100s were later purchased to make landings less dangerous in airborne stunts. A Triumph scooter was also used for a few comedy routines.

The riders wore blue breeches with a two-inch red leg-stripe, blue patrol jackets, black boots with white hose tops, black gauntlets with white cuffs, white waist belts and a helmet in the blue and white colours of the RCCS. The TRWs were army green while the Tigers were royal blue.

On tour, twenty riders total went with the two Tattoo teams and thirty-one with the Display Team. The Display Team covered 18,500 miles during 1967, visited ninety-six communities and performed before 550,000 people, from Courtenay, BC, to St. John's, Nfld.

Although well rehearsed, the performances were not without danger. Accidents happened, mostly in the privacy of practice, and one death occurred while the initial team of the 1950s was en route to a show in Winnipeg. A multiple-bike pileup on Manitoba's Highway No. 1 just outside Portage La Prairie was attributed to an eighteen-foot-long pothole in the pavement, an obstacle even these stunt riders found impassable.

**Roy Rogers and Dale Evans trade their horses for a Triumph Trophy to pose with the RCCS Motorcycle Display Team at the Canadian National Exhibition, Toronto, Ontario, August 1954.**

**A member of the Canadian Provost Corps Motorcycle Team soars through the air aboard a heavy Harley-Davidson. This early-pattern WLC was over twelve years old during the team's 1955 tour.**

**Two riders of the Canada West Tattoo practice their skills using a hybrid Triumph. The Trophy chassis, with its superior suspension, is mated to a slow-revving TRW engine, a combination well suited to the demands of the precision rides.**

**The Canadian Armed Forces Motorcycle Display Team in full dress uniform perform the pyramid at Parliament Hill, 26 July 1967.**

## CPL BILL WILKINS

RCCS

Bill Wilkins joined the army in 1953, a non-rider. Two years later, he stood in awe, watching the RC Signals DR Display Team perform. Never before had he seen such incredible stunts performed on motorcycles. When the show ended, Wilkins signed up for DR training.

Unfortunately, the Display Team was soon retired. Aside from training and army exercises, the military motorcycle was primarily a dust collector at this point. The annual exercise at Gagetown, New Brunswick, was one of the few instances where Wilkins was able to make use of his newly acquired motorcycle training.

"Billy Beals and I were out in the training area on a night-riding exercise. In blackout, you can see absolutely nothing other than a small light, so as opposed to riding the normal daytime speed of fifty miles per hour, you're down to twenty-five to thirty miles per hour, or maybe a little more if you were pretty sure you knew the road.

"We had stopped to have a cigarette when we heard this rumbling noise. There weren't supposed to be any tanks in the training area, so obviously the tank commander didn't know where he was. We started up our bikes and off we went. All of a sudden, I heard a crash. Billy had run into the tank! With his bike lying on the ground in a million pieces, he jumped up onto the tank and banged on the turret. When the tank commander opened the top, Billy said, 'Anybody hurt in there?'''

From the late 1950s to the 1970s, most official DR work was carried out using jeeps. Wilkins travelled to the Congo and Egypt, where he drove the four-wheeler, occasionally

**Above: Cpl Bill Wilkins achieves his goal of riding with a military Motorcycle Display Team at Vimy, Kingston, Ontario.**

getting shot at as part of the UN Peacekeeping Forces. His motorcycle only saw infrequent use back on native soil. It took Canada's one hundredth birthday and the resurrection of a Canadian Armed Forces Motorcycle Display Team to change that.

This was the opportunity Wilkins had only dreamed of—to be part of an outfit like the one he had witnessed more than ten years earlier, participating in the same sort of act that had coaxed him onto a bike in the first place. This was his outfit.

"We really didn't have any expertise. The original motorcycle DR Display Team of the 1950s was a takeoff on the British army DR Team. Murray Long was shipped back from Germany at the time because he knew the most about stunt riding. He was the only one with past experience. He instructed the instructors, because, other than occasionally doing a wheelie, which was taboo in the military, that was about the only stunt anyone else had ever done."

Training was rigorous: up at six in the morning, breakfast, physical training between seven and nine, and then the handful of experienced DRs would teach the inexperienced the basics.

"Prior to actually performing the stunts, after the initial bike-riding stages, we took them into a training area—cross-country riding. Hills, valleys, ditches, sand pits, ninety-degree drop-offs.

"After basic training, we started riding on the parade square. The first stunt everybody had to learn was how to ride sitting backwards on the handlebars with no hands. You get the bike wound up, set your throttle, sit on it backwards and let the clutch go. The first couple of times, you wind up sitting on the ground with the goddamn bike taking off down the field! Run it back, fire it up, get on it again, and stay with it.

"Mind you, there were victims laid by the wayside. In the first six months, we had something like over forty-five broken bones! We didn't really have any bad accidents during the year of training, nothing like broken necks and things like that.

"We started off with 120 people and wound up with 80. There was skill; there was size. What we wanted ideally was an individual who was in top physical condition. There was call for maybe three small people on the team; the top men of the pyramid. The remainder of them had to be 150-185 pounds ideally, but certainly not over 200.

"We had people cry because they wanted to be part of the team so bad and they tried so hard and they lost so much weight but they just could not get down to the basic physical requirements. I know for a fact it used to break Captain Jack's (Capt Jack Burman) heart to have to tell these individuals, 'Look, we're sorry.'

"You had objectives which had to be met. Basic training, riding backwards, riding on the handlebars backwards, riding frontwards on the pegs with no hands, etc. You'd turn down your steering damper so that it was snug enough to manipulate the bike with your weight.

"The performance area was eighty by one hundred yards. This was the area we had asked to have fenced off from the spectators. You had to learn how to ride within those dimensions without using your hands. If you didn't, you would be right into the crowd.

"We wore the high, lace-up motorcycle riding boots, riding breeches made of wool with the laces in the sides, a riding jacket, which was like a battle dress jacket, a helmet, riding gauntlets and goggles. We wore a pair of coveralls over this because it was easier to replace them than a pair of riding breeches.

"It was not a case of just teaching an individual to ride a motorcycle, or to be daring. You had to have trust in the others. You had to maintain your machine. When you are driving at high speeds and relying on another's dexterity on a motorcycle, and he is lacking, whether it be nerve, knowledge or experience, or just lack of maintenance and his machine fails . . ."

Before and after riding his machine, each rider had to run through 105 separate maintenance inspections and report any anomalies to the team mechanic.

Of the graduating riders, ten went with the red train and ten with the blue train to ride with the Tattoo, which left the rest to tour the country as the Motorcycle Display Team. And that was just the riding members. They also had two forty-foot tractor-trailers, two staff cars, a truck and a bus, a maintenance crew of about ten, and "chaps who didn't quite make the team but wanted to be part of it.

"There was no nucleus. Every rider on that team had to be able to perform if not all the stunts, then 30 out of the 35 or 40 rides. There was a total of 25 or 26 stunts, and you could not be a member of the team if you could not ride the majority of them. I knew 21, which was the norm.

"After training, the instructors and students both performed in the shows as equals. Some of these young fellows could do stunts that I could never dream of doing, simply because of their age, dexterity and willingness. But 60 percent of the riders that did the more difficult stunts had previous bike-riding experience, either in the military or in civilian life."

Of the many who volunteered for the team, preference was shown to experienced riders for instructors. For the rest, they wanted youth. The average age of the team was close to twenty. Because of the high level of skill required to perform the various stunts, the best of the graduates stayed with the Motorcycle Display Team (instead of the Tattoo).

"People had specific jobs. I was in charge of the maintenance logs on the team. Myself and another rider recorded every pint of oil, gallon of gas, or whatever that we went through. I was also leader of one side of the precision riding team. There were two sides, an A and a B."

Both the Display Team and the Tattoo boasted of intricate precision rides; what separated the teams was the stunts. The Display Team did leaps and the fire jump and the go-cart jump and much more. The human leap was considered by many to be the most spectacular. Fourteen people would lie down, then one rider would speed off a ramp, jumping over the bodies. Under the ramp was another team member. With only two hand grips, it was this soldier's job to hold that ramp in place as the weight of the rider and machine charged over, hopefully clearing himself and all his buddies behind him. The fate of fourteen soldiers literally rested in his hands.

"One close call, I believe it was in Calgary, the chap who was holding the ramp lost his grip as the bike hit the ramp. The ramp tilted to one side. Fortunately, the rider noticed, got the throttle on, and landed on an angle, just barely clearing the last body, Captain Jack.

"The go-cart ramp, we had a hell of a time with the go-cart, to build one that would work." The go-cart had a ramp built onto its front. It would start off at one end of the field while a motorcycle started at the other. When the two met in the middle, with both vehicles still in motion, the motorcycle mounted the ramp and "the bike just shot over top."

And there were card games in motion. Four men sat on a bike, seats on each side, with the front man riding backwards. "He'd just sit down and deal out a hand and they'd actually play cards while they were driving around. One would yell 'Euchre!' and the fans would roar.

**Cpl Dennis Stow of the Centennial Display Team and his Triumph Tiger 100 burst through the wall at sixty miles per hour. Although the bricks were made of balsa wood, the impact at speed was still severe.**

"And we had a sidecar that came apart. The rider would turn a corner and the sidecar would just continue on toward the crowd, with the guy in the sidecar waving frantically at the rider. It was a lot of fun.

"The pyramid was started from a standing start. When the last guy was on, he'd holler 'Okay, let her go!' You have three positions of throttle lock: idle, semi, and fast idle. You would set them on middle idle, and stay in line with the middle rider. When turning, the inside guy has to brake harder than the outside guy. We never fell in one performance.

"In training, many times, a guy's bike would take off, and the top guys would end up lying on the pavement behind us.

"We had a sixteen-man precision ride which reached speeds up to, well . . . we weren't supposed to exceed thirty-five miles per hour, but many times on pavement we'd get up to sixty miles per hour. The figure eight, the cross-over, the oohs and aahs of the audience—you were caught up in the momentum. I don't think there was any one of us who ever looked down at the speedometer.

"It looked difficult. But the timing was key."

The touring schedule was tight, sometimes leaving little opportunity for rest between performances. And rest was often not the first thing on the minds of this busload of young soldiers when arriving in a new town. Weariness diminished control; reaction time faded.

"We had gone into our ride, it was on grass, and a rider missed his hole. What I mean by that is, when you are in the figure eight, you start off as two separate lines of eight and you do a crossover, and then begin to circle around. You know from practice who your man is, so you are not looking at the circle, you are looking for your man to come around the corner. You just miss the back of his pannier with your crash guard and ride through the hole.

"Now, one mistake, if somebody blows it, we were always told to break off. Then once one driver was missing, the whole thing stopped. Timing was critical.

"We had just come out of the figure eight, when suddenly, two guys were flying through the air! Somebody had skidded out a little bit on the turn, and instead of backing out, tried to make it. He got hit right in the middle and both riders went down. He ended up with about twenty-some odd stitches."

That was the team's only injury in 132 performances during the four-month tour, although it was not their only accident. When travelling from Gagetown to Chatham, New Brunswick, in October, the team bus hit a moose. Fortunately, no one on the bus was hurt. The moose, however, did not fare as well. Team members bled the dead animal on the spot and the meat was donated to a local orphanage.

Every team member performed in every performance. Wilkins rode in the mass rides, the precision rides, the stand-up ride: "I had a guy leaning out between my legs and I rode standing up with no hands." Out of the twenty-five stunts, he rode in about seven of them at each performance, occasionally filling in for others on sick leave.

"The biggest thrill we got was the very first show we put on in Kingston at Norman Rodgers Airport. The largest crowd was at Winnipeg when we appeared at halftime during the football game. We were on national TV that time."

A full house in Vancouver included about thirty members of the Satan's Choice. "The cops were there, and the tension level was high because nobody knew what to expect. As it turned out, they had nothing but praise for the riders. They actually came up and shook our hands! The guy was standing there with beard down to here and hair down to his shoulders saying, 'Hey man, you guys are crazy!'

"The team worked like a one-man unit. It is hard to believe that never in the whole time that we travelled across this country did we have one single fistfight.

"We stayed at hotels, motels, bases, tents, whatever was available. You had all your clothing to transport with you, maintenance on the bikes every night, load the machines up, unload the machines—it was work!

"The Motorcycle Display Team did a fantastic job of public relations for the armed forces. And the comradeship. You could never replace those moments with anything. Every show resulted in a standing ovation. It was fantastic."

At the end of the tour, the team was disbanded and the bikes put into storage. Wilkins never got on a bike again.

The two-wheel drive Rokon at Val Cartier, Quebec, October 1969.

When the display teams of 1967 returned to Kingston after the centennial road show, a telegram was received from Canadian Forces HQ congratulating them on their efforts. Although it was hoped that the team would stay on as a permanent unit, it was disbanded at the end of the year in keeping with Canada's new policy of reducing its forces personnel. For many, 1967 was seen as the last hurrah for the Canadian military motorcycle.

Two years later, as if to reinforce this belief, the Canadian Forces HQ deemed that the stock of TRWs in storage was excessive. Several of these motorcycles were still in the original shipping crates, never having been unpacked or assembled. Many of these, plus any machine with over five hundred miles on the odometer was ordered disposed of. Permission was granted to all units to replace the bikes if a need was there. Few did. During October of the same year, the DND tested a two-wheel drive Rokon but no purchases were made. Inventory in 1973 showed 140 motorcycles in central storage and only 15 in active service.

Interest was revived when Bombardier began production of military motorcycles during the late 1970s. As Canada's sole motorcycle manufacturer, it is possible that some pressure was on the Canadian military to support the company's efforts, but for whatever reasons, Canada began to acquire new bikes from the small Valcourt, Quebec, producer.

The bike, known simply as the Bombardier Military Motorcycle, came in four two-stroke displacement sizes; 125, 175, 250 and 400 cc. It was based closely on the company's civilian Can-Am TNT street-trail bike, a fast, sturdy, agile and reliable machine. In 1977, Canada purchased approximately seventy-five of the 250 cc model Bombardiers. Both Britain and Belgium followed suit with larger orders in the early 1980s. Riders used to the TRW were amazed at how responsive and easy the Bombardier was to ride. With this model, the military motorcycle took a giant leap forward, finally abandoning Second World War technology in favour of contemporary efficiency and competence.

An early production Can-Am, the model upon which the Bombardier Military Motorcycle was based, is tested by a member of the Canadian Airborne Regiment during Exercise Oasis Caper, Mojave Desert, California, October 1973.

**The 250 cc Bombardier Military Motorcycle during an exercise at CFB Gagetown, NB.**

**The Bombardier proved a major leap forward in military motorcycle design, a fact these DRs training at Lahr, Germany, took full advantage of.**

# CPL RUSSELL BARTON

## 2nd Service Battalion, CAF

Russell Barton joined the Canadian Forces in 1981, and at the time of this writing was a corporal serving with the 2nd Service Battalion (2 SVC BN), Transportation Company. He got his DR training during Rendezvous 85, a major exercise held in 1985 near Wainwright, Alberta. In conjunction with this exercise, Barton's Company ran an eleven-day motorcycle course consisting of basic maintenance and plenty of dirt riding. Barton was one of five riders who participated, two as instructors and three as students.

"During our day rides, we would play rooster. A rider would steer into a mud swamp and gun the engine, shooting a rooster tail of mud and debris onto the person behind. I preferred to ride near the back of the pack, so needless to say, I had to stop many times to scoop the mud from my half closed eyes. We got soaked. Lots of fun."

One of Barton's fellow students acquired the nickname "Dozer" due to his inclination toward using his helmet for ploughing a furrow into the dirt whenever he fell. "We were all young, and it was fun falling."

Everyone fell at least twice a day during training. Barton's worst came after bragging about an accident-free morning. His Bombardier "discovered an old trench." When the dust settled, Barton's chin needed eight stitches to patch it up, leading to his new title of Scarface. "You can hardly notice it now."

The motorcycle training course completed, Barton returned to his company as the platoon warrant-officer's driver. The 2nd Service Battalion was entering the tactical stage of the exercise, and the company's two DRs were already chosen. "Once my truck was

**Above: A military police rider experiences no difficulty finding the mud at Exercise Rendezvous 85, CFB Wainwright, Alberta, 3 June 1985.**

**A tree serves as a suitable place to prop a wet Bombardier and hang the drenched clothing of Cpl Russell Barton.**

camouflaged, I had plenty of free time, so I made myself seen quite often by the higher-ups, hanging around the bikes and talking to the riders."

Fortunately for Barton, one of the riders sprained an ankle. "This was my chance. I stuck close to the bikes, and while the other rider was out on an errand, I was asked to take a message to Logistic Operations [Log Ops]. This was the start of my DR'ing.

"There were two field exercises back-to-back. The last one was nine days long. For those nine days straight, it rained." It seemed to Barton that every time he climbed aboard his bike, the storm was at its peak. "Seeing as I was the younger and more eager of the two DRs attached to the main Log Ops, I tried to ride as much as possible. With my military half-helmet, a scarf wrapped around my ears, nose and mouth, an oversized rain suit taped at the ankles so the water wouldn't go up my legs, and my forever-wet combat boots, I looked like an orphan looking for a home."

When not riding, Barton and his fellow DR, Steve Jones, spent those soggy days in a hutchy just behind the Command Post (CP). "A hutchy is two ground sheets put together, strung up between two trees. It is only hip high, so you have to crawl in and out."

For the first run, they flipped a coin to determine who would get drenched. "Happily, it was me. I was to take a message around to all the units that we supported. All their positions were marked on a big map, but you can't mark them on your own map in case you get captured. So instead of being given exact locations, I had to find them within a familiar grid square. The only way of knowing where they were was to spot someone's helmet sticking out of the ground or bushes.

"Zoom, there goes a helmet. I got the bike stopped and turned around and pulled up to the soldier. 'Hi, are you 2 RCR?' 'Nope, the Patricias.' I could have sworn the Patricias (PPCLI) were still up the road ten more kilometres. Oh well."

A trio of DRs cruise along the trails of CFB Wainwright, Alberta, during Exercise Rendezvous 85.

Barton headed into the bush, struggling over several fallen trees and slugging it out through puddles and mud holes, eventually locating the company CP. "I trip into the CP and hand my message to a young Captain. He reads the message with a puzzled look on his face, and asks, 'Are you sure this is for us?' 'It sure is if you're PPCLI.' 'Well, I guess it's not for me then. This isn't PPCLI.' This news wasn't the most pleasing part of my ride. After that, I made sure the sentry identified his unit code."

Barton found riding in Wainwright, Alberta, fairly easy because of the many tank trails and cut lines. "Usually, we did two runs daily to the rear to deliver messages and pick up mail. I eventually found an almost direct route; about half a kilometre on the road, down a large section of trail, across the road and down another tank track."

After five days, the battle moved forward about forty kilometres, taking the two DRs along. "We set up our hutchy a little further from CP this time. Steve and I both needed a good sleep. Five minutes after our sleeping bags were laid out, we were out too. About two hours later we heard, 'Hey guys, we need a suicide jockey inside!'" Barton lost the coin toss again.

"It was daybreak by now. I had to deliver a message to the helicopter squadron." As this squadron was located in the same area where the killer trench attacked Barton and cut his chin, he was already familiar with the terrain and what surprises it might hold. "The rain had stopped, but it was still very dreary. I rode off wondering what ever possessed me to want to be a DR. Once I felt the bike under me and the wind and mud in my eyes, I remembered.

"On the northwest part of the map is a bridge called Battle River Bridge. Across the river is a series of hills, followed by an almost ninety-degree climb. On our DR course, we spent a lot of time trying to climb this hill, so I knew what to expect. Once past the first few hills, the next one is a good jump hill. I gassed her (as any good rider does) and found myself aboard an airborne motorcycle. Oh no, PEOPLE! By the time I hit the ground, I had both brakes on and the bike in second gear. Then I recognized the CO, Colonel Gates."

Unwittingly, Barton had interrupted a planned ambush. Yet neither this nor his dropping in unexpectedly on the colonel deterred him, for the mail must go through. "Leaving the CO, I still had the monster hill ahead to climb. I had tried this hill before and not fared too well, usually bogging out halfway up or flipping over backwards. Now, I had lost all my speed but figured I could still make it. And I did, charging up the hill, gearing the bike like an old vet. It felt good knowing that there was little left that could stop this DR."

Getting close to home is always a good feeling, even if home is only a hutchy. The mind tends to relax. "Having seen enough water to last me a lifetime, I was riding back to CP, trying to avoid the mud puddles. That turned out to be the biggest mistake of my day. All of a sudden, my front tire was up on the grass and I was in a high-speed slide. Before I knew it, I was flying. Then gravity took over. I ended up sitting straight-legged on the road facing the same direction I had been travelling, with my motorcycle behind me poised perfectly on her handlebars and seat.

"The bike wouldn't start, so I walked her back to camp, figuring she needed a rest, which was true. Half an hour later, we were both on the road again. What a life!"

**The chipping olive-drab paint on this Honda Trail 90 lasted about as long as the Canadian military's interest in this bike.**

Around the same time as Bombardier's entry into the military vehicle market, the Canadian military purchased two Honda Trail 90s for appraisal in use with airborne units. Even though the chrome trim and bright orange frame and body parts of this diminutive trail motorcycle were covered in regulation olive drab, it was not deemed suitable for military use. The bikes are now collecting dust in the Canadian War Museum warehouse.

In 1983, declining motorcycle sales and increased competition from the Orient in the civilian market caused Bombardier to farm out production of its motorcycles to Armstrong Competition Motorcycles of England. This move did little but postpone the inevitable. The Can-Am name, and therefore Bombardier's association with motorcycling, ended in September 1987. The last contract for Bombardier Military Motorcycles, with the Belgian army, had been filled during 1982.

But Armstrong picked up where Bombardier had left off with military bikes. Using four-stroke engines made by Bombardier's Rotax division in Austria, the British company developed prototypes in 1984 of a 500 cc military motorcycle known as the MT500. Canada and Britain began replacing Bombardier 250s with production versions of the newer and more powerful MT500. Then in October of 1987 came the surprise announcement that Harley-Davidson had purchased the world rights to the Armstrong MT500. Canada's supplier of military motorcycles is once again Harley-Davidson.

Canada's remaining Bombardiers and the newer MT500s continue to see limited use in Canadian Rendezvous (RV) and NATO exercises, plus some limited DR work, the latter role principally in Europe by outfits like the RCHA Regiment stationed in West Germany.

Motorcycles are slowly seeping back into military service throughout the world. Since the beginning of the twentieth century, the motorcycle's dependence upon rider skills has been both its strongest asset and its downfall. A bad rider will only hurt himself. A good rider can make a motorcycle go through amazingly tough terrain very quickly. It is not a weapon, nor can it successfully be combined with one, as history has shown. Yet when it comes to mobility, and assisting in the movement of land-based weapon and soldier convoys, nothing has ever proven to be superior.

**The Armstrong MT500, now manufactured by Harley-Davidson.**

# APPENDIX A
# CANADIAN MILITARY MOTORCYCLE SPECIFICATIONS

| **Manufacturer** | Clyno (AJS)<br>(UK) | Douglas<br>(UK) | Indian<br>(USA) | Triumph<br>(UK) |
|---|---|---|---|---|
| **Period** | 1914-18 | 1914-18 | 1914-18 | 1914-18 |
| **Model** | 5-6 HP | V | Powerplus | H |
| **Engine** | 744 cc<br>side valve<br>V-twin<br>5-6 hp @ 2,500 rpm | 350 cc<br>horizontally<br>opposed twin<br>2.75 hp | 1,000 cc (61 ci)<br>inlet over exhaust<br>valve V-twin<br>7 hp | 550 cc<br>side valve single<br>4 hp |
| **Ignition** | magneto | magneto | Dixie magneto | magneto |
| **Carburetion** | one | one Amac | one Wheeler or<br>Schebler | one Triumph |
| **Suspension:**<br>front<br><br>rear | <br>friction dampened<br>horizontally sprung<br>rigid | <br>friction dampened<br>parallelogram<br>rigid | <br>trailing link<br><br>rigid | <br>pivoted girder<br><br>rigid |
| **Brakes:**<br>front<br>rear | <br>caliper<br>drum | <br>caliper<br>block | <br>none<br>drum | <br>stirrup<br>block |
| **Tires:**<br>front<br>rear | <br>both<br>3.50 x 26 | <br>both<br>2.25 x 26 | <br>both<br>3.00 x 28 | <br>both<br>2.50 x 26 |
| **Wheelbase** | 59 in (1499 mm) | 53 in (1346 mm) | 59 in (1499 mm) | 52 in (1321 mm) |
| **Weight** | 300 lb (136 kg) | 200 lb (90.7 kg) | 353 lb (160 kg) | 201 lb (91 kg) |
| **Transmission** | 3-speed handshift | 2-speed handshift | 3-speed handshift | 3-speed handshift |
| **Top speed** | 50 mph (80 km/h) | 35 mph (56 km/h | 55 mph (88 km/h) | 45 mph (88 km/h) |
| **Notes** | Used with the Motor Machine Gun Corps. The armour plated sidecar mounted a Vickers machine gun. | A larger Model B was built for sidecar use. 18,000 V and B models supplied to Allied Forces. | Used by the Canadian Expeditionary Force in Canada and England. | 300,000 supplied to Allied forces. Affectionately dubbed "Trusty Triumph" by troops. |

| **Manufacturer** | Birmingham Small Arms (BSA) (UK) | Harley-Davidson (USA) | Scott (UK) | Triumph (UK) | Triumph (UK) |
|---|---|---|---|---|---|
| **Period** | 1933-43 | 1930-38 | 1930-38 | 1938-39 | 1938-39 |
| **Model** | J12 | VL | Flying Squirrel | Tiger 90 | Speed Twin |
| **Engine** | 500 cc<br>OHV (overhead valve)<br>V-twin | 1,200 cc (74 ci)<br>side valve<br>V-twin<br>28 hp @ 4,000 rpm | 600 cc<br>water cooled<br>two-stroke twin<br>24 hp @ 4,000 rpm | 500 cc<br>OHV single<br>28 hp @ 5,800 rpm | 500 cc<br>OHV<br>vertical twin<br>28.5 hp @ 6,000 rpm |
| **Ignition** | magneto | coil | magneto | magneto | magneto |
| **Carburetion** | one Amal | one Schebler | one Amal | one Amal | one Amal |
| **Suspension:**<br>front<br>rear | girder<br>rigid | leading link<br>rigid | girder<br>rigid | girder<br>rigid | girder<br>rigid |
| **Brakes:**<br>front<br>rear | both drum<br>7 in (178 mm) | both drum | both drum | both drum<br>7 in (178 mm) | both drum<br>7 in (178 mm) |
| **Tires:**<br>front<br>rear | both<br>3.50 x 19 | both<br>4.00 x 27 | both<br>3.25 x 19 | both<br>3.25 x 19 | 3.25 x 19<br>3.50 x 19 |
| **Wheelbase** | 58 in (1473 mm) | 59 in (1499 mm) | 51 in (1295 mm) | 52.5 in (1323 mm) | 52.5 in (1323 mm) |
| **Weight** | 365 lb (165 kg) | 401 lb (182 kg) | 353 lb (160 kg) | 320 lb (145 kg) | 360 lb (163 kg) |
| **Transmission** | 4-speed footshift | 4-speed handshift or 3-speed plus reverse | 4-speed footshift | 4-speed footshift | 4-speed footshift |
| **Top Speed** | 65 mph (105 km/h) | 90 mph (145 km/h) | 65 mph (105 km/h) | 75 mph (120 km/h) | 80 mph (130 km/h) |
| **Notes** | Used by RCAF ground crews in the Middle East during WWII. | Supplied as solo or with various sidecars attached. Interchangeable wheels, reverse gear an option. | Used by the Non-Permanent Active Militia in the 1930s. | Both the Tiger 90 and The Speed Twin were used by the PPCLI for Royal Escort Duty in 1939. | |

## APPENDIX A

| Manufacturer | Associated Motorcycles Ltd. (UK) | Birmingham Small Arms (BSA) (UK) | Indian (USA) | Indian (USA) | Norton (UK) |
|---|---|---|---|---|---|
| **Period** | 1939-45 | 1939-45 | 1939-45 | 1939-45 | 1939-45 |
| **Model** | Matchless G3/L | M20 | Scout 741B | Chief 340B | Big 4 |
| **Engine** | 350 cc<br>OHV single<br>16 hp @ 5,600 rpm | 500 cc<br>side valve single<br>13 hp @ 4,800 rpm | 500 cc (30.5 ci)<br>side valve V-twin<br>15 hp @ 4,800 rpm | 1,200 cc (74 ci)<br>side valve V-twin<br>36 hp @ 4,500 rpm | 634 cc<br>side valve single<br>15 hp @ 4,500 rpm |
| **Ignition** | magneto | magneto | coil | coil | magneto |
| **Carburetion** | one Amal 275/1 | one Amal 276 | one Linkert or Schebler | one Linkert or Schebler | one Amal |
| **Suspension:**<br>front<br>rear | <br>telescopic<br>rigid | <br>girder<br>rigid | <br>girder<br>rigid | trailing link<br>leaf spring<br>spring plunger | <br>girder<br>rigid |
| **Brakes:**<br>front<br>rear | <br>both drum<br>5.5 in (140 mm) | <br>both drum<br>7 in (178 mm) | <br>both drum | <br>both drum<br>6.75 in (171 mm) | <br>both drum<br>7 in (178 mm) |
| **Tires:**<br>front<br>rear | <br>both<br>3.25 x 19 | <br>both<br>3.25 x 19 | <br>both<br>3.50 x 18 | <br>both<br>4.00 x 18 | <br>both<br>4.00 x 18 |
| **Wheelbase** | 54 in (1372 mm) | 54 in (1372 mm) | 57 in (1448 mm) | 61.5 in (1562 mm) | 54.5 in (1384 mm) |
| **Weight** | 328 lb (149 kg) | 369 lb (167 kg) | 450 lb (204 kg) | 575 lb (261 kg) | 679 lb (307 kg) with sidecar |
| **Transmission** | 4-speed footshift | 4-speed footshift | 3-speed handshift | 3-speed handshift | 4-speed footshift |
| **Top Speed** | 70 mph (113 km/h) | 60 mph (97 km/h) | 65 mph (105 km/h) | 80 mph (130 km/h) | 50 mph (80 km/h) |
| **Ground clearance** | 6 in (152 mm) | 4.5 in (114 mm) | 5 in (127 mm) | 5 in (127 mm) | 5.5 in (140 mm) |
| **Notes** | First motorcycle with telescopic forks to be used by Allied Forces. | 126,334 units manufactured, or about one quarter of combined Commonwealth Forces motorcycles. | Some shipped with metric instruments. Front and rear wheels interchangeable. | Used by Canadian Forces in Canada and England, many with sidecars attached. | 3,300 units built during WWII. Sidecar wheel was driven, the unit often equipped with a Bren gun. |

| Manufacturer | Triumph (UK) | Ariel (UK) | Royal Enfield (UK) | Excelsior (UK) |
|---|---|---|---|---|
| **Period** | 1939-45 | 1939-45 | 1939-45 | 1939-45 |
| **Model** | 3HW | W-NG | CO | Welbike |
| **Engine** | 342 cc<br>OHV single<br>17 hp @ 5,200 rpm | 346 cc<br>OHV single<br>17 hp @ 5,000 rpm | 346 cc<br>OHV singe | 98 cc Villiers Jr. Deluxe<br>two-stroke single<br>1.5 hp |
| **Ignition** | magneto | magneto | magneto | magneto |
| **Carburetion** | one Amal | one Amal 275 | one Amal | one Villiers |
| **Suspension:**<br>front<br>rear | girder<br>rigid | girder<br>rigid | girder<br>rigid | rigid<br>rigid |
| **Brakes:**<br>front<br>rear | both drum<br>7 in (178 mm) | both drum<br>7 in (178 mm) | both drum<br>6 in (152 mm) | no front<br>rear drum<br>4 in (102 mm) |
| **Tires:**<br>front<br>rear | both<br>3.25 x 19 | both<br>3.25 x 19 | both<br>3.25 x 19 | both<br>2.25 x 12.5 |
| **Wheelbase** | 52.5 in (1334 mm) | 56 in (1422 mm) | 53.5 in (1360 mm) | 39.5 in (1003 mm) |
| **Weight** | 316 lb (144 kg) | 354 lb (159 kg) | 316 lb (144 kg) | 70 lb (32 kg) |
| **Transmission** | 4-speed footshift | 4-speed footshift | 4-speed footshift | one-speed |
| **Top Speed** | 60 mph (97 km/h) | 70 mph (113 km/h) | 60 mph (97 km/h) | 30 mph (50 km/h) |
| **Ground clearance** | 6 in (140 mm) | 6 in (140 mm) | 5 in (127 mm) | 4 in (102 mm) |
| **Notes** | Limited numbers produced as the Triumph factory had been destroyed during a 1940 bombing raid. | This was the most numerous WWII military motorcycle produced with an OHV engine. | The CO was occasionally used by RCAF ground crews. | Designed to fold-up into a 15 in dia. container with a parachute, this small bike was used for ground movement of paratroops. |

APPENDIX A

| Manufacturer | Norton (UK) | Harley-Davidson (USA) | Triumph (UK) | Bombardier (CDN) | Armstrong/ (UK) Harley-Davidson (USA) |
|---|---|---|---|---|---|
| **Period** | 1939-56 | 1939-56 | 1956-69 | 1977-85 | 1985- |
| **Model** | 16H | WLC | TRW | Military | MT500 |
| **Engine** | 500 cc side valve single 13 hp @ 4,800 rpm | 750 cc (45 ci) side valve V-twin 25 hp @ 4,500 rpm | 500 cc side valve vertical twin 18 hp @ 5,000 rpm | 247 cc Rotax rotary valve two-stroke single 26 hp @ 7,500 rpm | 500 cc Rotax overhead cam single 32 hp @ 6,200 rpm |
| **Ignition** | magneto | coil | magneto alternator | Bosch electronic | electronic |
| **Carburetion** | one Amal 276 | one Schebler | one Solex SU | one Bing | one Amal 29/30 |
| **Suspension:**<br>front<br>rear | <br>girder<br>rigid | <br>bottom link girder<br>rigid | <br>telescopic<br>rigid | <br>telescopic<br>swingarm | <br>telescopic<br>swingarm |
| **Brakes:**<br>front<br>rear | <br>both drum<br>7 in (178 mm) | <br>both drum | <br>both drum<br>7 in (178 mm) | <br>both drum<br>6 in (152 mm) | both drum<br>5.5 in (140 mm)<br>6.3 in (160 mm) |
| **Tires:**<br>front<br>rear | <br>both<br>3.25 x 19 | <br>both<br>4.00 x 18 | <br>3.25 x 19<br>4.00 x 19 | <br>3.00 x 21<br>4.00 x 18 | <br>90/90 x 21<br>4.00 x 18 |
| **Wheelbase** | 54.4 in (1383 mm) | 57.5 in (1461 mm) | 53 in (1346 mm) | 55 in (1397 mm) | 57 in (1445 mm) |
| **Weight** | 367 lb (166 kg) | 550 lb (250 kg) | 366 lb (166 kg) | 287 lb (130 kg) | 353 lb (160 kg) |
| **Transmission** | 4-speed footshift | 4-speed handshift or 3-speed plus reverse | 4-speed footshift | 5-speed footshift | 5-speed footshift |
| **Top Speed** | 65 mph (105 km/h) | 65 mph (105 km/h) | 72 mph (114 km/h) | 70 mph (112 km/h) | 104 mph (167 km/h) |
| **Ground clear-ance** | 5.5 in (140 mm) | 4 in (102 mm) | 6.5 in (166 mm) | 9 in (230 mm) | 8.7 in (220 mm) |
| **Notes** | The "Snortin" Norton" and the Harley-Davidson proved to be the most popular motorcycles among Canadian military personnel. | 10,000 shipped from Canada, 44 with sidecars. Interchangeable front and rear wheels. | 11,512 manufactured for all NATO Forces, plus 4,415 spare engines. | By 1981, 71 were in service with Canadian Forces. | 85 purchased by the Canadian Forces in 1985. |

## APPENDIX B: CONTRIBUTORS

### INDIVIDUALS

Adams, Clair
Aisbitt, Jack
Alexander, Bill
Andrews, Ron
Baitman, Melvin
Bannerman, Hugh
Barham, Frank E.
Barnes, Bill
Barton, Russell
Beauchesne, Clem
Bennes, Bert
Bennes, Glen
Benson, Denis
Berton, Pierre
Brault, Norm
Brooks, T.
Brown, R. A.
Brown, Robert F.
Brown, Ronald S.
Bryer, Jack
Budgen, Gord
Bullman, B. H.
Burman, Jack
Burnlees, Dee and Bill
Caldwell, Bill
Cameron, Eric
Cameron, Ruth
Caron, Leno J.
Clarke, Stephen
Comeau, Mike
Conway, Jim
Corbeil, Sylvan "Stan"
Craig, John
Cuthill, George K.
Davis, Frank 'Tex'
Dawson, Dennis
Dawson, Ollie
Desgagne, Albert
Dextraze, J. A.
Donnelly, T. S.
Doody, Don
Doran, Bill
Drummond, Mac
Duhaime, Gladys
East, Stewart
Elliott, George
Ercolini, James
Essex, James
Fice, W.
Fleck, Jim
Foster, G. S.
Gagnon, Fred
Gaiger, Art
Gibson, Fred
Gibson, Roland
Goddard, Howard
Gore-Langton, B.
Grancola, Armand
Greer, Gilbert
Hardwick, Clarence
Hargreaves, Bill
Harvey, Ernie
Haughey, Vic
Haughton, Tom
Hine, George
Hodgson, G. B.
Hollington, Leslie
Holowachuk, Brock
Humphrey, Ken
Hunter, Pauline
Jeffery, Tom
Jones, Merv F.
Johnson, Al
Johnson, Don
Josefowich, Mike
Kasanda, Jerry and Margaret
Kerr, Cecil "Red"
Lalonde, D.
Lanigan, J. P.
Lapointe, L. J.
Lehman, Ray
Lewis, Carl
Libby, Richard
Liscumb, Larry
Lowson, Allan
MacDonald, Rodger
Makin, David
Marshall, George
Marshall, Kenneth Roy
McDermid, Rita
McKie, Bert
McLaughlin, Arthur
Meadows, George
Meads, J. W. Wally
Michaud, Louis
Millard, John
Montgomery, Alex
Morrison, Angus
Mount, Ernie
Nelson, Conrade
Newell, J. C.
Nicholson, Bernie
O'Connor, Ed
Paget, Norm
Perry, J. L.
Phipps, Mary
Picknell, Art
Pineo, Bill
Priestley, George
Puckett, J. Howard
Redman, Stanley
Reeve, Bruce
Richardson, Bernard
Ridler, Russ
Ritchie, Gordon
Ritchie, Howard
Robinson, Mary
Robotham, Robert
Rogers, Emerson
Roker, L. J.
Rowland, T. W.
Russell, George
Russell, Howard
Sawatsky, Dick
Shanks, Ossie
Shanks, Reg
Shortt, Bill
Sigmond, Robert
Simms, Elmer
Smith, C. E. "Bud"
Smith, James
Smith, Pat
Sparrow, Vic
Speller, Lionel
Stephenson, Dave G.
Stevens, Colin
Storey, W. E.
Theriault, Bert
Tranter, Ralph
Turner, W. E. (Wally)
Veldheer, Peter A.
Walker, Rex
Walton, Glenn
Welch, Tom
Wilding, Scotty
Wilkins, Bill
Williams, Donald
Young, Morley
Yull, Ralph

APPENDIX B

## MUSEUMS AND ARCHIVES

Bunker Museum, Cobalt, Ont.
Canadian Airborne Forces Museum and CFB Petawawa Military Museum, Petawawa, Ont.
CFB Borden Military Museum, Borden, Ont.
Canadian Forces Communications and Electronics (CFCE) Museum, Vimy (Kingston), Ont.
Canadian Forces School of Intelligence and Security Museum, CFB Borden, Ont.
CFB Gagetown Military Museum, Gagetown, NB
Canadian Military Engineers (CME) Museum, Chilliwack, BC
Canadian War Museum (National Museums Canada), Ottawa, Ont.
Imperial War Museum, London, England
Le Musée Royal 22è Regiment, La Citadelle, Que.
Maritime Command Museum, Halifax, NS
Motorcycle Museum of Canada, Edmonton, Alta.
Museum of the Royal Westminster Regiment, New Westminster, BC
Provincial Archives of Alberta, Edmonton, Alta.
Provincial Archives of Manitoba, Winnipeg, Man.
Public Archives of Canada, Ottawa, Ont.
Public Archives of Ontario, Toronto, Ont.
Public Archives of Prince Edward Island, Charlottetown, PEI
Regimental Museum, PPCLI, Calgary, Alta.
Royal Canadian, Artillery Museum, Shilo, Man.
Royal Canadian Regiment Museum, London, Ont.
Saskatchewan Archives Board, Regina, Sask.
Seaforth Highlanders Museum, Burnaby, BC
York University Archives, *Toronto Telegram Collection*, Toronto, Ont.
Yukon Archives, Whitehorse, Yukon

## OTHERS

*Air Force Magazine*
*Canadian Defence Quarterly*
Canadian Forces Photographic Unit
Canadian Forces School of Intelligence and Security
Canadian Vintage Motorcycle Group (CVMG), *Gerald Barker Collection*
Canadian Women's Army Corps Association
*Classic Bike Magazine*
*Classic Motor Cycle Magazine*
*Cycle Canada Magazine*
*Maroon Beret*, 1st Canadian Parachute Battalion newsletter
National Defence HQ, Directorate of History, Director of Information Services
Railton's Photography Limited
Royal Canadian Legion
Royal Canadian Mounted Police (RCMP Quarterly)
*Sentinel, Magazine of the Canadian Forces*
*Thunderbird Journal* (CAF Military Police)

# NOTES

## THE FIRST WORLD WAR

1. Col A. J. Kerry and Maj W. A. McDill, *The History of the Corps of Royal Canadian Engineers*, Vol. I (Ottawa: The Military Engineers Association of Canada, 1962) p.170.

2. David Minton, "Bikes in Battledress," *The World of Motorcycles, An Illustrated Encyclopedia*, (N.Y., N.Y: Columbia House, 1977) Vol. 9, p.1017.

3. Col W. W. Murray, *The History of the 2nd Canadian Battalion (East Ontario Regt, CEF)*(Ottawa: Mortimer Press Ltd., 1947), p.239.

4. Murray, p.256.

5. Kerry and McDill, p.236.

6. Kerry and McDill, p.236.

7. R. Raife, "Tommy Atkins A-Wheel" (London, England: n.p., 1917), p.134

8. Charles Deane & Brian Crichton, *The Pictorial History of Motorcycling* (London, England: Octopus Books Ltd., 1982), p.156.

9. Kerry and McDill, p.141, 236.

10. Kerry and McDill, p.253.

11. Bert's son, Glen Bennes, carried on the family tradition and became a DR in the latter stages of the, Second World War because "I liked motorcycles." Unfortunately, most of his work was carried out in a jeep or armoured car.

## BETWEEN WORLD WARS

12. Prepared under the direction of the Chief of the General Staff, Army HQ, Ottawa, *Canadian Army Training Pamphlet, The Training of Motorcyclists* (Ottawa: Queen's Printer and Controller of Stationery, 1932), p.5.

13. General Staff, p.5.

14. General Staff, p.6

15. Col. G. W. L. Nicholson, *The Gunners of Canada, The History of the Royal Regiment of Canadian Artillery* (Toronto: McClelland & Stewart Ltd., 1972), p.19.

16. Carden managed an automotive garage owned by Loyd. Together, they designed the Carden Loyd Mark VI, which became the standard machine-gun carrier for the Commonwealth Forces between the wars. (H. Rogers, *Tanks in Battle, The Imperial Services Library Vol. VIII* (London: Seeley Service & Co. Ltd., 1965), pp. 84-85.

## THE SECOND WORLD WAR

17. By the 1931 Statute of Westminster, Newfoundland was recognized as an independent dominion within the British Commonwealth. It was not until 1949 that Newfoundlanders chose, by ballot, to join the confederation of Canada.

18. Department of National Defence, *Canadian Army Training Memorandum, No. 6* (Ottawa: Queen's Printer, 1941), p.51.

19. *The Flèche, Vol. X, Issue* #2 (Islington, Ontario: Islington United Church Newspaper, September 1970), p.1.

20. R. Munro, *Gauntlet to Overlord, The Story of the Canadian Army, 2nd ed.* (Toronto: The MacMillan Co. of Canada Ltd., 1946).

21. Chief of the Imperial General Staff, *Training of Motor Cyclists, Military Training Pamphlet No. 24* (Ottawa: Printer to the King's Most Excellent Majesty, 1939), p.1.

22. Imperial General Staff, p.7.

23. Chief of General Staff, *Regulations for Drivers of M. T. Vehicles, Universal Carriers and Motorcyclists* ("Not to Be Published," 1943), p.59.

24. G. L. Cassidy, *Warpath, The Story of the Algonquin Regiment, 1939-1945* (Toronto: Ryerson Press, 1948; rpt. Cobalt: Highway Book Shop, 1990), pp. 125, 129.

25. W. Churchill, *The Grand Alliance* (Boston: Houghton Mifflin Co., 1950), p.177.

26. "Citation," *Award of the Military Medal to K83926, Cpl L. C. Speller, RCCS* (courtesy of the Hong Kong Veterans' Association, BC Branch).

27. T. Allen, *Motorcycle Sport* (October, 1975), p.406.

28. G. W. L. Nicholson, *The Gunners of Canada* (Toronto: McClelland & Stewart Ltd., 1972), p.66.

29. During the summer of 1987, Leno Caron and his wife rode from Toronto, Ontario, to Winnipeg, Manitoba, on their Honda Gold Wing. The purpose of the tour was to visit Morley Young, a friend of Leno's last seen "dead" in 1945, rediscovered alive through their separate letters written as contributors to this book.

30. *The Daily Mirror* (London, England: Thursday, August 20, 1942), p.8.

31. G. L. Cassidy, *Warpath,* p.116

32. L. H. Nicholson, "Battle Dress Patrol," *RCMP Quarterly, Vol. 12, No. 3,* (January 1947), pp.232-249.

33. Col. G. W. L. Nicholson, *The Canadians in Italy* (Ottawa: Queen's Printer, 1966).

34. Nicholson, *Italy*, p.640.

## APPROACHING A NEW CENTURY

35. HQ US Army Field Forces Board No. 1, *Evaluation of Motorcycles, Appendix M* (Fort Bragg, NC, June 28, 1951).

36. Quoted from RCCS promotional literature given to local journalists prior to each RC Signals Display Team Performance.

## GLOSSARY

| | |
|---|---|
| AC2 | Aircraftman II Class |
| ACV | Armoured Command Vehicle |
| ADMS | Acting Director Medical Services |
| ADS | Advanced Dressing Station |
| Artificer | Skilled in a trade, mechanic |
| A-Sgt | Acting Sergeant |
| Btn, BN | Battalion |
| CAB | Canadian Armoured Brigade |
| CAF | Canadian Armed Forces |
| CASF | Canadian Active Service Force |
| CCS | Casualty Clearing Station |
| CEF | Canadian Expeditionary Force |
| Cement Head | *see* CSM |
| CFB | Canadian Forces Base |
| CMAC | Canadian Motor Ambulance Corps |
| CMHQ | Canadian Military Headquarters |
| Coy | Company |
| CO | Commanding Officer (OC is also used, usually WWI and earlier) |
| CP | Command Post |
| Cpl | Corporal |
| CRE | Canadian Road Engineers, colloquial of troops, officially RCE |
| CSM | Company Sergeant Major, "Cement Head" |
| CTS | Canadian Training School |
| CWAC | Canadian Women's Army Corps |
| DDMS | Deputy Director Medical Services |
| Div | Division |
| Double Duty | Performing more than one duty, the additional duties, such as picket duty, guard duty or kitchen duty, usually assigned as punishment |
| DRLS | Despatch Rider Letter Service |
| DR | Despatch Rider |
| Fd | Field |
| FDS | Field Dressing Station |
| Fitter | Mechanic |
| F-O | Flying Officer |
| Gelignite | High explosive |
| Gen | General |
| Gnr | Gunner |
| HQ | Headquarters |
| LAA | Light Anti-Aircraft |
| LAC | Leading Aircraftman |
| LAD | Light Aid Detachment (recovery of vehicles) |
| L-Cpl | Lance Corporal |
| L-Sgt | Lance Sergeant |
| LCT | Landing Craft, Tank |
| Lt-Col | Lieutenant-Colonel |
| Maj-Gen | Major-General |
| M/c | Motorcycle |
| MD | Medical Director |
| ME 109 | German WWII single engine fighter aircraft |
| MT | Motor Transport |
| NAAFI | Navy, Army, Air Force Institute (canteen, social centre) |

| | |
|---|---|
| NATO | North Atlantic Treaty Organization |
| NCO, non-com | Non-commissioned officer (warrant officer, sergeant, corporal) |
| NPAM | Non-Permanent Active Militia |
| OC | Officer Commanding (CO is also used, usually post WWI) |
| ORs | Other Ranks |
| Part I Orders duties, | A posted bulletin announcing a military unit's news, coming events, promotions, canteen hours, special events, etc. |
| Pointsman | A Provost or DR dismounted and directing traffic |
| POW | Prisoner of War |
| PPCLI | Princess Patricia's Canadian Light Infantry |
| Pte | Private, lowest ranking soldier |
| QM | Quarter Master (in charge of stores and materials) |
| RAF | Royal Air Force |
| RCA | Royal Canadian Artillery |
| RCAF | Royal Canadian Air Force |
| RCASC | Royal Canadian Army Service Corps |
| RCCS | Royal Canadian Corps of Signals |
| RCE | Royal Canadian Engineers |
| RCEME | Royal Canadian Electrical and Mechanical Engineers |
| RCHA | Royal Canadian Horse Artillery |
| RCMP | Royal Canadian Mounted Police |
| RCOC | Royal Canadian Ordinance Corps |
| RCR | Royal Canadian Regiment |
| Recce | Reconnaissance |
| Regt | Regiment |
| Sapper | Lowest ranking soldier in the RCE, equivalent to a private |
| S&T | Supplies and Transport |
| SDR | A DR delivering important and restricted messages to general field officers, general staff at HQ or to the chief of staff. |
| Sgt | Sergeant |
| Sigmn | Signalman |
| Sqn | Squadron |
| Stonk | Bombardment with artillery, also used to describe bombardment with alcohol (excessive drinking) |
| Subaltern | 2nd Lieutenant |
| WD | War Department |

# INDEX

(Figures in boldface refer to photographs)

# PHOTOCREDITS

Owing to space limitations, the following abbreviations have been used:
CME: Canadian Military Engineers Museum
CFCE: Canadian Forces Communications and Electronics Museum
CVMG: Canadian Vintage Motorcycle Group
DND: Department of National Defence
NAC: National Archives of Canada
PAO: Public Archives of Ontario

## THE EARLY YEARS

Page 9: Camp Silhouette Series No. 10, Photochrom Co. Ltd., London, Eng.

## THE FIRST WORLD WAR

Page 11: L. Keene, National Museums of Canada; 12 :T.W.W.; 12 :CME Museum; 13 :CFB Borden Military Museum; 14 :Imperial War Museum; 16 :Provincial Archives of Manitoba, H. W. Winkler Collection; 17: CFB Borden Military Museum; 22 :Imperial War Museum; 23 :E. Mount, Jr.; 24 :CFCE Museum; 25: NAC; 26 :B. Bennes; 28: PAO.

## BETWEEN WORLD WARS

Page 30 :S. Cameron, Provincial Archives of Alberta; 32 :DND/CFCE Museum; 33 :Regimental Museum, PPCLI; 34:CME Museum.

## THE SECOND WORLD WAR

Page 35 :Alex Colville, Cdn War Museum; 36 :F. Royal, NAC/DND; 36 : A. M. Stirton, NAC/DND; 37 : A. M. Stirton, NAC/DND; 38 :DND; 38 :York University Archives, Toronto Telegram Collection; 39:A. M. Stirton, NAC/DND; 39:B. Nicholson; 40 :B. Nicholson; 41 :H. G. Aikman, NAC/DND; 42 :NAC; 45 : Cooper, NAC/DND; 45 : Cooper, NAC/DND; 46 :L. J. Lapointe; 49 :Pat Smith; 51 :D. Lalonde; 52:T. Jeffery; 53 :O. Shanks; 55 :Cdn Forces Photographic Unit; 55 :E. Cameron; 56 :L. Liscumb; 57 :RCMP; 57: F. Dubervill, NAC/DND; 58 :RCMP; 59 :Imperial War Museum; 61 :A. Gaiger; 63 :K. Humphrey; 65: Art Picknell; 65 :B. Nicholson; 66 :J. Aisbitt; 68 :F. Dubervill, NAC/DND; 70 :Cdn Forces Photographic Unit; 71 :L. Batchelor, National Gallery of Canada; 72 :E. Rogers; 74 :P. Veldheer; 75 :P. Veldheer; 76: Alex Colville, Cdn War Museum; 78 :J. H. Smith, NAC/DND; 79 :A. M. Stirton, NAC/DND; 79 :J. Ercolini; 80: R. Lehman; 81: Captain Console, Imperial War Museum; 82 :Cooper, NAC/DND; 83 :R. Cameron; 84 :F. Royal, NAC/DND; 85 :CFCE Museum; 87 :M. Young; 89 :C. Nelson; 90 :K. Bell, NAC/DND; 91 :L. Caron; 93 :D. Guravich, NAC/DND; 98 :CFCE Museum; 102 :NAC/D. MacKay Collection; 103 :K. Bell, NAC/DND; 103 :NAC/DND; 104 :J. Smith, NAC/DND; 105 :J. Smith, NAC/DND; 106 :Anderson, National Museums of Canada; 108 : T. Rowe, NAC/DND; 111:N. Brault; 112 :C. Nye, NAC/DND; 113 :T. Rowe, NAC/DND; 115 :DND/CFCE Museum; 118 :J. Smith, NAC/DND.

## APPROACHING A NEW CENTURY

Page 119 :DND; 120 :C. E. Nye, NAC/DND; 121 :P. Plastow, NAC/DND; 122 :NAC/DND; 122 : NAC/DND; 122 :NAC/DND; 122 :NAC/DND; 122 :NAC/DND; 122 :NAC/DND; 123 :W. Olson, NAC/DND; 123 :DND/Cdn Forces School of Intelligence and Security; 124 :F. Davis; 125 :M. Burns; 126 :York University Archives/Toronto Telegram Collection; 127 :DND/CFCE Museum; 128 :N. Turofsky, CFCE Museum; 129 :DND/CFB Borden Military Museum; 130 :Saskatchewan Archives Board; 131 :A. Porter, DND; 132 :Saskatchewan Archives Board; 135 :DND/CFCE Museum; 137 :Cdn Forces Photographic Unit; 137 :J. Rodger, Cdn Forces Photographic Unit; 138 :Cdn Forces Photo; 139 : Cdn Forces Photo; 140 :V. Johnson, Cdn Forces Photo; 141 :R. Barton; 142 :V. Johnson, Cdn Forces Photo; 144 :W. Storey; 145 :DND.